A T[illegible]artha

To [illegible] your promotion
to Young Peoples Bible Class.
May you grow in the
knowledge of Jesus Christ
and find Him to be your
true friend.

Yours in His name
Mrs. Lindasleye
(on behalf of S.S)

A Thoroughly Modern Martha

The Life of Brigadier Martha Field

by

MARY ENDERSBEE

HODDER AND STOUGHTON
LONDON SYDNEY AUCKLAND TORONTO

ISBN 0 340 20124X. *Printed in Great Britain for Hodder and Stoughton Limited, Mill Road, Dunton Green, Sevenoaks, Kent, by Cox & Wyman Ltd, London, Reading & Fakenham.*

Contents

Foreword

Martha Field was the last person to want a book written about herself. Like her biblical namesake, she got on with the job of 'caring for folks', without a thought about seeing her name in print. It is significant though, that on several occasions her dedication did hit the headlines in the local and national press. This book, therefore, is intended as a tribute to the many hardworking goodwill officers of The Salvation Army whose names have never made their way into the papers. To tell the story it has been necessary in places to change certain names.

There are many people whose help and encouragement made this book possible — not least Martha Field (now Mrs. Lt.-Colonel Martha Osborne) herself. Among the many I should thank are a host of Martha's friends and colleagues, and in particular Winnie Bewick, Sophie Wilson, Brigadier Gladys Taylor and Brian Hart. I am grateful too for the advice and support of Commissioner Kathleen Kendrick of The Salvation Army's Literary Department.

MARY ENDERSBEE

1

'Just Look What You've got us Lassies Into!'

It is Christmas 1965 in one of the poorest districts in Britain — St. Ann's, Nottingham. The late afternoon gloom is occasionally relieved by a shopwindow decorated with fairy lights or a tinsel-laden tree. Otherwise the inadequate street lighting does little to alleviate the murkiness. The sadly neglected terraced houses, and narrow alleyways of one-up one-down hovels do not bear close inspection.

A sudden splash of light falls across the sloping cobbles at the top of a narrow incline as the front door of a sturdily-built, detached house opens. A woman is entering and the outside light, switched on to signal to the neighbours that the occupant is home, will remain on when the door is shut. The light reveals the woman is wearing the navy blue uniform of a Salvation Army officer and her oval, spectacled face and dark hair are framed by the distinctive bonnet with its bow at the side. She is Brigadier Martha Field, a Salvation Army Goodwill Officer, and the house she has entered in Storer Street is a Goodwill Centre, where spiritual and material help is offered in God's name, to all in need.

The light reflects on the broken windows, flaking paintwork and crumbling brickwork of the nearby doss-house. Its neglected fabric shelters some fifty down-and-outs, vagrants, alcoholics, meths drinkers and drug addicts.

The light casts a deep shadow where the front door of the doss-house stands permanently open. Into that shadow lurches one of the occupants. From his behaviour and his dishevelled clothing it is clear that he is under the influence of some addiction. After a few moments of swaying uncertainty, he staggers away down the dark slope.

The quiet of the deserted street gives a false impression of peace. How long before the addict returns is hard to say, but his return is accompanied by the frightened panting cries of a young girl whom he is dragging along by the arm. They are only a few feet from the dark chasm of the doss-house door now, and the girl is screaming, 'No! No! Let me go!', as she is dragged inside.

Suddenly the door of the house with the light outside flies open. Martha Field runs as fast as she can down the steps, followed less speedily by a man. She is across the cobbles and straight in the dark doorway before he has reached the road. A few seconds and a shout or two later she reappears and the young girl is carried across the street in the safety of the man's arms.

One backward glance reveals that the thwarted addict has staggered back to the doorway of the doss-house. But the girl is safe now. The trio mount the front steps of the Goodwill Centre. The door shuts. The addict sways and curses in the doorway opposite. The light shines on in the darkened street.

It is twenty-four hours later. The street looks much the same, and the same small determined figure in navy blue appears around the corner. Brigadier Martha Field is returning from the Post Office, an old lady's pension stored safely in the depths of her bag.

If the truth be known, she climbs the narrow uneven pavement apprehensively. The man from the doss-house had been loitering when she left home and the previous night he had smashed the windows of the next house. 'I do hope he's gone,' Martha thinks. 'Soon be home now anyway. Though there's no one in at the centre by the look of things. Captain must still be out distributing parcels . . .'

As she reaches the gateway and turns in, the man, knife in hand, steps out of the shadows and bars her way. Martha, unable to escape, is forced to retreat up the path, until she is pinioned against the wall.

'I might as well go for something big, then,' the man mutters threateningly, moving the knife towards Martha's throat, which is so tightened by fear she cannot speak. She watches the tip of the knife coming nearer. The metal catches in the zip-front of her tunic and slowly he runs it down as if contemplating his next move.

'Lord, help me!' Martha prays, now silently intent on edging her way up the path. 'If I can only reach the steps . . .' Her foot finds the first one and she summons up sufficient courage to make a hasty dive up the rest and in the door, slamming it behind her with relief. The man's battering goes unheeded as she shoots the bolts home and stands leaning against the wall facing the picture of the Salvation Army's Founder, William Booth.

'Just look what you've got me into,' she says to his thin face with its deep-socketed eyes. But her admiration for William Booth's Christian dedication to the poor, the unwanted, the unlovely, the needy, steadies her. Hadn't she wanted, from her earliest days, to serve others as her childhood heroine, Florence Nightingale, had done?

* * *

'This is a picture of Florence Nightingale called "The Lady with the Lamp" — she is moving down the rows of sick and dying soldiers from the Crimean war. It is because of her determination and courage that we have hospital nurses and district nurses today . . .'

'Oh my! Isn't she wonderful—fancy doing that?' thought young Martha Field as she gazed adoringly at the picture the teacher was pinning on the classroom wall. For almost as long as she could remember she had wanted to be a nurse—just like her heroine. She could imagine herself in a starched white apron with a red cross sewn to its bodice, and with her first aid bag over her arm tending the sick. Even now, her mind drifted away from the rest of the lesson, because soon it would be going home time and she would be able to go to the shop that sold remnants.

She felt in her pinafore pocket for the hankie in which the precious pennies she had saved were tied. Yes, it was still there. Her eyes strayed again to the big classroom clock . . . Then the clang of the handbell sounded and they were dismissed. Running, laughing, shouting, the children poured out of the gates of the Church of Ireland Junior school in Belfast and past the sandbagged front of the school building. Martha looked quickly over her shoulder to see if her younger brother Leslie was following her. No, he was going in another direction, running home to Somerset Street with his pals.

With her pretend 'first aid bag' safely over her arm she ran the other way. The sooner she and her friends reached the shop the better, for they wanted plenty of time to play before curfew at nine o'clock.

The people who ran the remnant shop were kindly and knew well Martha's smiling oval face. They also knew the bargain bundle of scrap material she was hoping to buy.

'Is it for dolls' dresses, you'll be wanting it, then?' asked the woman at the till, as she put the end-cuts off the various rolls into a paper bag.

'Oh, not for dolls' dresses,' Martha said. 'It's for nurses' uniforms—aprons and caps for me and Annie here.' She struggled with the knots around the pennies. 'And then we'll make some for our dolls — an' the left-overs we'll tear up into bandages.'

'There now! You'll never get all that out of just these, to be sure,' the woman laughed. 'Here, have an extra piece for luck.'

Somerset Street, off the Ormeau Road, Belfast, where Martha Field was born in 1911 was a typical working class road of terraced houses with three bedrooms, two of which were tiny. Downstairs there was a large front room and a small back scullery leading into a small yard with an outside lavatory and dustbin. Martha's parents considered themselves fortunate to have water and gas piped to the house for in some areas people still had to rely on pumps and well water, and cooked on an open range.

The district housed many of the workers in the huge thriving Belfast industries of shipbuilding and linen spinning. The year Martha was born saw the opening of the city's Thompson Graving Dock. In 1910 Belfast could claim to have more linen spindles operating within her boundaries than any other country in the world. Though Martha was blissfully unaware of it she was a citizen 'of no mean city'.

As Martha neared home she thought about the changes that had taken place there. She had her own bedroom now, for her elder sister, Jessie, had sailed away down Belfast Lough to a new life in Canada. All Martha knew about Canada was that in winter it was extremely cold, and had lots of snow. She wasn't quite sure why her sister wanted to go there. And she knew it had been a wrench for her parents. But Jessie was twenty-one and free to make up her own mind.

She knew also that she would find her mother at home preparing tea for her, Joe and Leslie. Father wouldn't be there because he would be at work, playing his clarinet or the drums in the orchestra pit of the Lyceum Theatre. Her heart lifted as she thought about her father, for he had promised to get tickets for the silent film being shown on Saturday and which he was accompanying. The film had Martha's favourite star, Charlie Chaplin. Sometimes Father managed to get seats for them to see live shows such as the Black and White Minstrels or Gilbert and Sullivan operas.

Martha loved music, but to her sorrow she seemed to have little talent. She knew Father had learnt to play his trumpet and clarinet in England as a bandboy in a military band when he enlisted in the British Army. He was obviously talented at a young age, but somehow it hadn't rubbed off on Martha. Father had gone with the Army to fight in South Africa and then come to Ireland to the big Military Camp at the Curragh in County Kildare.

Returning to civilian life he settled in Belfast, and established himself as a professional musician. Martha knew their family would never be rich, but if their home was humble, it was happy with simple things like laughter and music and teasing — and holidays at the seaside.

* * *

When she was eleven, Martha went up to the 'big' local Methodist School. She had always enjoyed learning, but practical things usually appealed to her more than theory. So after history, came singing and cooking. Both her Grandma and her mother were excellent cooks, and Martha delighted in learning how to make soda bread, griddle scones and puddings.

She loved singing, not only at school but also on Sundays. In the Field household, as in many others in Belfast, Sunday was different. Families with any self-respect sent their children to Sunday school and there were huge classes in the many Belfast churches. The Field children, in their Sunday best, went to the nearby Church of

Ireland Sunday school. Martha loved the hymns. 'Holy, holy, holy, Lord God almighty' particularly impressed itself upon her and remained a favourite all her life.

One Sunday in 1923 a new attraction vied with Sunday school. Down on the open ground, which Martha passed on the way back from church, was a small group of people, men and women in navy blue uniforms. It wasn't what they were wearing that caught her attention but the lovely catchy music they were making with a concertina and a tambourine. She lingered, listening to the words. It was some sort of hymn, but not quite like anything they'd had at Sunday school where a tinny piano was played ponderously by a woman member of the church.

As she hesitated, the man with the concertina closed it up and the group bowed their heads. A man's voice carried to Martha quite clearly. He was praying and as they finished she heard a resounding 'Amen'. The man with the concertina smiled round as the group broke up, and catching sight of Martha, to her surprise, approached her with an invitation to attend the children's meeting in the Salvation Army hall at Ballynafeigh, the following week. Martha knew that Ballynafeigh Corps wasn't too far from her home, so she said shyly that she would like to come but would have to ask her parents.

No-one at home had any objections when Martha bounded in with the news that a kind man from The Salvation Army had asked her to attend one of their children's meetings. The Salvation Army was well-known in Belfast, having nine corps in the city, and carrying on a work in the slums of Ballymacarrett. So Martha's parents, nominal churchgoers, were not worried about her attending.

Martha set off to her first Salvation Army children's meeting the following week and enjoyed the games and the singing especially. She learnt that there was a meeting for young people on Sundays and determined to go. The lure of the music and the friendliness of the lady in charge, called the Young People's Sergeant Major, drew her back week by week. She continued to attend regularly, drinking in the challenge that was explained to the children on Sundays by the young Captain. Her heart was stirred by the call of Jesus Christ to repent and follow Him.

One Sunday, when the appeal was made for any who wanted to come to the Mercy Seat, she knew she must go forward. As Martha knelt there, the officer came to kneel with her, and in a few moments of quiet conversation and prayer, she helped Martha to ask God to forgive her in Christ's name, and cleanse her for future service for Him.

Martha was thirteen, and full of youthful enthusiasm for her new-found faith. She loved every moment spent with her friends at Ballynafeigh and was keen as could be to qualify as a corps cadet, though she knew she would probably have to wait a long time to save enough money to buy the proper uniform. In the meantime she was told she could come in a navy skirt and a red jumper. The officer's memories of Martha at this time are of a gay happy youngster with an abundance of enthusiasm, and a care for people.

Martha's parents noticed her keenness with tolerance, though her brothers thought her silly! There was no attempt to stop her, and with the time drawing near for her to leave school, they resolved to watch how she would cope with life outside the confines of home and classroom.

For Martha there were mixed emotions as she looked ahead to leaving school. She still longed to be a nurse but in the end unforeseen circumstances took the matter out of her hands and limited her choice of a job. In July 1924 her father suffered a severe stroke which left him almost completely paralysed. Life in the Field home was never quite the same again.

First they had to move a bed downstairs for her father who needed to be spoonfed and tended in every way. Then her mother had to go out to earn money. She was fortunate in finding a cleaner's job at the local school. Martha, in her turn, had to be responsible for her father's tea while her mother was at work. Each afternoon she would rush home to feed him. The neighbours were kind, dropping in when they knew everyone was at work, to see that father was all right.

Martha also learnt the art of listening at night for Father, alert to any sounds that might mean he needed help. This capacity was to stand her in good stead in the years ahead.

It was obvious that the sooner Martha left school the better it would be for the family finances. Nursing was definitely out of the question.

The sweet-making factory employing between 150 and 200 people seemed a happy enough place. Martha enjoyed her job of packing sweets. In the lunch-break she would hurry home and get her father's lunch. If there was a rush order for sweets, she would go back to do a couple of hours' overtime.

The only evenings she tried to keep free were those when the Salvation Army corps cadets met to study the Bible and learn how to work as Salvationists. She loved every moment, happiest when an opportunity arose to help with young children. Her admiration for the officers in charge of the work increased, as she saw their loving devotion to others. Perhaps Florence Nightingale's image was beginning to fade a little now, and in its place came a young Salvation Army officer caring for the needy. But whenever Martha's thoughts drifted in that direction she pushed the idea away. She felt she would never make the grade and qualify for training.

In 1928, after four years of sickness, Martha's father

died, and all that seemed worthwhile went out of her life. What was to happen to them now? How could she ever leave her mother at home to train as an officer?

At the Army hall the new Captain comforted a distraught Martha and gave her hope, reminding her that if her call was real, God would find a way. She encouraged her to forget her problems in serving others and Martha, having experienced sorrow and death, was able to reach out in a new way to those in need. It was the new Captain who helped Martha to put on her first proper Salvation Army uniform, guiding her fumbling fingers as she tried to tie the bonnet ribbons into the right kind of bow.

Mrs. Field viewed her intentions with less enthusiasm. She had never kept Martha from going to the Army, but with her husband's death she naturally leant harder on her younger daughter's help, loath to see her leave home. Martha, for her part, was torn in two; she wanted to help her mother but her deepest longing was to go to London for officer training — if despite her fears, she could be accepted for the college. She wanted to serve God in serving others — young children, old people, the sick and the needy.

Finally all her pent-up longing crystallised one day as she read about the work of the Army slum officers in the hopfields of Kent and Worcestershire . . . During the hop-picking season the officers lived with the workers and looked after the very young children helping with first aid and hot tea for the pickers. There was a photograph of some of the slum sisters in their huge white aprons with their tea-urn on a wheelbarrow. It was just what Martha longed and believed she should be doing.

'There — that's what I'm going to do, one day,' she said to her mother, showing her the picture in the issue of *The Young Soldier* she had been reading. Her heart sank as her mother's face registered disapproval.

'Now, Martha, you just forget that . . . There's plenty for you to be doing here.'

Martha knew her mother was right, yet in spite of every obstacle, the call of God gripped her with such strength that in 1929, when she had been attending the Corps for five years, she felt she had to respond. One Sunday morning she went forward to the Mercy Seat to dedicate herself to God as a sign that she wished to become an officer. She turned for advice to the Captain.

'Do you think I ought to be an officer?' Martha's concern was evident and sincere. The Captain's reply was not quite what she expected.

'Not unless you really have to,' she said quietly, leaving Martha in some doubt as to what she meant. Despite her perplexity Martha knew she must press on. Her every longing to serve God and those in need seemed to be driving her forward to become a Salvation Army officer.

Perhaps Captain's less than enthusiastic response had been to make quite sure that impulsive Martha knew what she was doing. Having appeared cool in her initial reaction, she gave Martha every encouragement to show herself worthy for cadet training. For a special task she suggested that Martha should sell *The War Cry* each week in a nearby village, Newtonbreda, and seek to bring the Christian gospel to the people she met there. It was up to Martha to find ways of doing that, and in her own practical way she did.

It took some courage at first. The eighteen-year-old Martha was a little frightened, for she had never been to the village or done anything quite like this door-to-door visiting before.

'Come away in then,' an elderly lady's voice called from a dim interior. Martha accepted the invitation, drawing out a copy of *The War Cry* as she did so, and smiling as she bent to introduce herself to the little old lady, with her long hair twisted up in coils around her head. There was an immediate sense of friendliness and soon they were chatting, sitting near the window. Martha's fears abated, for this experience was repeated as she visited other homes.

In Salvation Army terms and to Martha these villagers were 'her people'.

2

Leaving Home

'But what is going to happen to your mother, Field? How is she going to manage if you go to college? You don't want her to end up in the workhouse, do you?'

'Oh no, Colonel,' Martha protested, aghast at the suggestion, 'There's my brother Leslie at home — he'll help to keep my mother. And there's Joe also who won't let her want.'

Under her Army bonnet Martha's pale tired face revealed the effort it had been to attend this, her first candidate's interview, at the Army's Divisional Headquarters in Belfast's Royal Avenue. She had a struggle to hold back the tears. For the Colonel had touched on the sorest point of all — her mother — and the impossible task she faced, if accepted, of leaving home against her mother's wishes. This struggle had made the whole interview more of a strain.

Unable to sleep Martha had risen very early, too nervous to eat any breakfast. Praying for God's will to be done, she had prepared herself, checking her appearance with special care. She set off to see the officers at the quarters at Ballynafeigh for moral support and encouragement.

Captain noticed at once how upset she was and soon had her sitting down to a cup of tea and some breakfast while they reassured her. She had felt a little better after that, yet here was Colonel Holmes confirming all her worst fears.

But the Colonel, though he had put the worst side to her, did relent enough to encourage her not to give up hope. The firm conviction Martha showed in speaking of her call was strongly in her favour. Then the warm recommendations from the officers at Ballynafeigh left little doubt that she was a suitable candidate.

At least two years, and two more interviews, were to elapse before, in 1934, Martha at last achieved her goal. Difficult years they were too — years of obedience and loyalty to her mother who still found it hard to understand Martha's desire to leave home. There were troubles enough in Belfast in the early thirties, and plenty for a keen young Salvationist to do there, without going over the water.

In the end, realising the depth of Martha's determination and longing, Mrs. Field gave her consent. In the summer of 1934 Martha sailed out of Belfast Lough for the first time in her life. She was crossing to Liverpool to take the train south to London and the Training College at Denmark Hill.

The awareness of all she was leaving behind hit her hardest as she looked back from the boat to see the familiar faces of loved ones and dear friends receding, and the green coastline of home fading into the distance. She went below, and took out the new Bible given to her by her Salvationist comrades. One of them had written on the flyleaf 'For I the Lord thy God will hold thy right hand, saying unto thee, fear not, I will help thee'. She read and re-read the words and felt comforted.

At first the newly-built college seemed to be huge, impersonal and overwhelming — a place of surnames, bugle calls and bells, of reading rules, having interviews and attending lectures. There were over 300 cadets in what was called the 'Awakeners' session, about 200 of whom were women. The cadets were accommodated in twelve 'houses', around a central quadrangle.

It was in House 2 that Martha found friendship and support to help overcome her initial homesickness and cope with ensuing crises. First she discovered a kindred spirit in Barbara, the Cadet in the very next room to her own. They shared a longing to do hopfield work — and hoped to become Goodwill Officers after training. They had both been challenged and inspired by reading *God in the Slums*, Hugh Redwood's account of his introduction to the Army's slum and goodwill work. They were both practical and found study difficult.

Far sooner than she expected Martha settled into the college's daily routine — bugle call at 6.30 a.m., prayers, a work section of house-cleaning before breakfast, a time of private prayer and Bible reading; then lectures and classes in the mornings, private study and practical work in the afternoons.

There seemed to be little time to relax, but once a week free time occurred when the cadets could look after their personal needs, go out of college shopping or to see the sights of London. It was seldom that Martha availed herself of this opportunity, for what little money she had saved was usually spent on necessities like books, stationery and fares.

As Christmas drew near the two Cadet friends shared their hopes and fears. They knew that after the recess they would be placed in one of three sections — slum or goodwill; social; corps work — and receive six months' special training for their future work. They both longed to know if the Army would confirm their own sense of God's calling for slum work.

Martha constantly doubted her suitability to be an Army officer let alone a slum sister. Though she had succeeded against fairly daunting odds to get to the training college, she still believed the Army might at any moment send her home.

In her darkest moments Martha came to appreciate the warmth and understanding of the Officer in charge of House 2. Adjutant Olive Williams was an attractive, auburn-haired woman with a vast capacity for picking up despondent cadets and setting them on their feet again. Often, after talking over her sense of inadequacy with Adjutant Williams, Martha felt, 'Yes. I can do it!'

At Christmas Martha and her friend, Barbara, were both assigned to Slum work. To Martha's particular delight their course now included special lectures on First Aid and Home Nursing, and they were prepared for the St John Ambulance Brigade certificate. There were also sessions led by officers experienced in slum and goodwill work and they had to study local government and civic affairs.

Slum work was not only service in a practical sense; the spiritual side of the work was given careful emphasis. Among the meetings Slum Officers would be expected to hold were Sunday evangelistic meetings for adults, Sunday school and week-night meetings for children, and Home League meetings for women.

In fact Martha was amazed at the wide variety of tasks a Slum Officer could be called on to perform — from running a youth club, serving 'meals on wheels', visiting the lonely and sick, helping families in distress, accompanying patients to hospital, cleaning up sickrooms or doing home nursing. From the very young to the very old — it was people in need who mattered most whether it was cooking meals and caring for children left temporarily without parents in an emergency, shopping, drawing pensions for the aged, or laying out the dead – as one officer commented, 'the Slum Sister has to bring an encyclopaedic knowledge to the problems of today'.

Some of these things Martha began to experience while at college in her weekly 'field work' but many of them she was going to have to learn to cope with 'on the job'. All the cadets were attached to a London corps or goodwill centre and Martha was thrilled to travel twice a week across the Thames to Hoxton in North London, where she was sent out visiting the old and young, and helped with the soup-run late at night for the down and outs. Every other Sunday she was there too helping with the meetings. It was her first real contact with the narrow dark terraced streets of London slums and her first experience of the cheerful cockney humour that enlivened them despite the dreadful conditions.

Sickness and disease had to be faced by those working in the slums. It was no use fainting at the sight of physical weakness or suffering. Martha had already nursed her father and knew a little, but some of the cases she visited and heard about were new to her. Cadets had to take extra care after doing field work. The Army provided each with a book entitled *Rules for the Guidance of Cadets* in which instructions about sick visiting were listed.

Remembering her early longing to do hopfield work, she hoped she would be appointed to an East End centre where she could accompany the pickers on their annual visit to Kent. The East End it was! On May 13th, 1935, Lieutenant Field read her first Marching Orders:

'I am pleased to inform you on behalf of the Commissioner that you are appointed as Assistant Officer to Bethnal Green Slum Post. You will proceed there on 16th May, and assist your Commanding Officer in every possible way to carry out the Orders and Regulations of the Army, for the glory of God and the Salvation of the People.'

Lieutenant Field packed her suitcase with mixed feelings: expectation that in her new post she would have the satisfaction of at last being properly 'on the job', trepidation that she might not prove worthy of her commission and be recalled. The first year was a probationary period she knew. Her sorrow at being separated from her friend, Lieutenant Barbara David, was softened by the knowledge that she too would be working in the London area at Paddington and they would be able to keep in touch.

Martha's first Slum Post was to be, like so many of the others, a converted public house. Number 40 Tagg Street, Bethnal Green, was a corner site with the downstairs 'bar' changed into a large room for meetings, a kitchen behind, and the officers' quarters upstairs, with two bedrooms, a sitting-room and bathroom. Though it was surrounded by narrow streets sandwiched between the Old Ford Road and Roman Road it was pleasantly decorated inside. Her Commanding Officer, Captain May Stewart, had been at the post for some eighteen months. The Slum Post was clean and bright, in stark contrast to some of its neighbours.

Captain gave Martha a warm welcome, but was well aware of her responsibilities towards her new assistant. She was determined that this 'green' young slum officer should begin her work as she meant to go on. It was a matter of pride to see that she brought out the best in her charge, and gave her a training that she would never forget. She kept Martha to the strict routine that the training college considered correct: early rising for personal private prayer and Bible study, breakfast, then cleaning of quarters and hall. Both Captain and Lieutenant were ready in uniform to be out visiting by 10.00 a.m. Lunch was taken at the quarters before the rest of the day's duties commenced: more visiting, a Home League meeting; children's Joy Hour, or possibly hospital visitation, or caring for a sick or aged person. Sundays saw the children coming to the hall for Sunday school and the adults for a meeting, while on Saturdays there was pub booming, and possibly an open-air meeting. Captain and Lieutenant were expected to attend the local army corps for the Sunday morning Holiness meeting. All officers of the area were responsible to the Divisional Commander at the Congress Hall, in Clapton.

Often as she hastened back to the quarters she was convinced that she was a failure as a Slum Officer, and she was not sure she could stand it. She was bitterly disappointed, for she had believed that once she was commissioned she was going to see lots of people converted, and she didn't. These were the worst moments she had experienced since offering herself for goodwill work. Had all her struggles been in vain? Perhaps it would be better to go home now, before the Army sent her?

Martha had to remind herself of the encouragement she had often found in talking to Adjutant Olive Williams at the college. She believed God had called her and therefore she had to believe 'I can do it.' It was this certainty that helped her through those difficult early months, as it was to help her many times in the future.

3

Hopfields – At Last!

'If you could just see me now. I'm in my glory!' wrote an exhausted but exhilarated Martha to her mother from the Kent hopfields. However depressed she had felt about her first few months in Slum work, the trip out of London to Cuxton had truly lifted her spirits. The dust, grime and smells of the narrow London streets were left behind and the fresh air and the soft green and blue of the heat-hazed rolling Kentish landscape welcomed them to the hectic three or four weeks' work among the pickers.

Here she was, busy from early morning till late at night and loving every moment. There were the babies and young children to care for and the cheerful backchat of their East End parents to cope with. The field boiler had to be filled and kept alight with stacks of wood, while there was the tea urn to take round on its barrow. Most important to Martha was the First Aid post, with its ample medicines and bandages. She was truly in her element here!

Their ranks were swelled from time to time by volunteers from local corps or from London, and senior officers from headquarters usually called in to help with special meetings. Sometimes it was a 'gospel raid' on the local pubs, where many of the pickers spent their money as fast as they earned it. Open-air meetings would be held in the warm evenings and one such remained vivid in Martha's memory for it was a stormy Saturday night when flashes of lightning danced on the glasses from which the men were drinking, before the rain fell in torrents and dispersed the gathering.

There was no doubt about it, though, the hopfield daily routine was tough. Up at 6.00 a.m., ready to take the children at 7.00 a.m. while their mothers went to work, making sure each child was given a name tag so that there were no muddles. Some of the children needed a good wash before being popped into Army-supplied rompers to kick and gurgle happily or sleep on straw pallets. Some, of course, would be fretful and need the watchful attention of the two girls in charge.

Collecting wood was almost a full-time occupation meanwhile. The big field boiler had to be filled and lit for washing dirty nappies, clothes or bodies. Its appetite for kindling was enormous. The tea urn also had to be primed and filled with strong, sweet tea – to be sold to the hot thirsty pickers at a penny a pint in jugs, billy cans, kettles, anything that they brought. A cake manufacturer supplied the Army with large slabs of madeira and fruit cake, which were cut up and sold at a penny a slice.

Martha's glory was definitely the First Aid post, stocked with syrup of figs, iodine, blue bag, aspirin, milk of magnesia, plasters, cotton wool and rolls and rolls of bandages. She never knew what to expect, though on the whole she dealt with fairly minor things like stings or bites, an occasional scald or burn from cooking over open fires, sunburn or the inevitable tummy troubles from eating or drinking unwisely. Now and again it could be far more serious, though Martha felt she was fortunate not to have to tend anything too difficult.

She had heard of one friend, also on the hopfields that year, who found herself a nervous assistant holding the oil lamp steady in the middle of the night, while Major tended a woman who was having a miscarriage on the straw pallets usually used by the children. As her arm ached more and more, her anxiety was whether she could keep the light steady and not drop the lantern altogether.

There was the far less serious story she'd heard of a very large woman coming to a First Aid post pulling along a small man.

'Major, I've brought my old man with 'is 'ead, 'e's 'ad it on and off for days and 'e's sittin' out there now, holdin' it in 'is 'ands! Will you give 'im a dose of that brown stuff?' She indicated the giant bottle of syrup of figs. The man was duly dosed.

Fire was probably the greatest hazard of all, for it spread through the camps with horrific speed. Dreadful accidents could occur and the Army workers tried to do what they could to aid the fire brigade, often managing to be first on the scene with their 'battery' water cart.

Normally, though, the smell of woodsmoke was pleasant, mingling with the tang of the hops and adding to the pleasure of the open air life, where hearty appetites from hard work, the healthy exhaustion of tired limbs and the flush of sunburn on pale skin, all made up the benefits of being on the front line with the pickers.

But there was the tough, rough side as well: the constant honking and revving of lorries, charabancs and cars in the narrow country lanes at all times of the night, and especially at weekends. Added to this was the drunken singing and rowdiness late into the evening, with the accompanying fights and brawls; the incredibly primitive conditions under which the pickers lived: airless, windowless sheds quite often, or barns with few sanitary facilities of any kind, and a general lack of hygiene. Hugh Redwood visited the Slum Sisters in action on the hopfields and commented 'If the picking of the hops lasted three months instead of three weeks the scandal of the hopfields would be physically impossible. Epidemics would ravage the camps, and the countryside would rise against the drunken debauchery to which its peaceful villages must now submit. As things are, the general attitude is that of the rider who puts his head down and plunges into the storm: it may be an inferno while it lasts, but it will soon be over.'

The Army plunged into the storm on the hopfields not only for the physical wellbeing of the pickers. The battle was waged on the spiritual frontline as well, and Martha threw herself into both warfares with vigour, struggling to keep up with the demands for food, drinks, medicines and cleanliness, while helping to run children's meetings and Sunday school, campfire sing songs, open-airs and evangelistic meetings, or just gossiping the gospel with the people who came to the First Aid hut or sought advice.

Soon it was time to pack up and put away the equipment, clear out the medicine shelves, and scour the tea urn and the field boiler in preparation for the return to London, to catch up on a little sleep before resuming the battle once again at Bethnal Green.

Martha's stipulated year at a London Slum Post (cut short to six months) soon passed and had an unexpected conclusion, for before 1936 had run its course, she was given her Marching Orders to go to Bristol with Captain May Stewart, who had been put in charge of the Slum Post at Bedminster.

Bristol had some likeness to Belfast, being much smaller than London and having port and shipbuilding industries along its waterfront. But the real sea air could be found only by those who made their way to Avonmouth by train or road, or by steamer down the River Avon from Hotwells. If the day was fine, many Bristol citizens took the steamer much further, all the way to Ilfracombe and back, watching the coastline of Somerset and North Devon slip by. Perhaps Martha longed one day to watch it from the boat home to Belfast—seeing places like Weston-super-Mare, Minehead and Lynmouth to the south, and the South Wales coastline with the Pembroke Peninsular to the north?

But it was those citizens of Bristol least likely to take a steamer anywhere whom Martha and her Captain had come to serve. The post in Wilway Street, like that in Tagg Street, was a converted 'pub' situated in the less salubrious part of the city. Bedminster was south of the River Avon and Bristol's dockland was not far away. The houses crowded shoulder to shoulder, with little sanitation, and not even gaslight in some places. Poverty and misery, courage and humour jostled each other. Despite the harshness of life, many people were brave and sacrificial.

The Bristol Slum Post had had quite a history, in fact, as Martha was soon told by some of their regulars. It had not always been in the converted 'pub' but had started its career in a room over a shop selling animal feed. There were some exciting tales of conversions too, including some men and women who had come to Christ through 'pub raids' carried out by the Slum Sisters.

At least one of their people could tell the story for herself, and Martha listened with wonder, to the vivid testimony of Mrs. Potts, whenever she had the opportunity. Mrs. Potts was a colourful local character. In her early days, she had been a heavy drinker often in deep trouble, beaten up in drunken brawls, frequently carried off to the police station. Her husband, in desperation, brought a crate of beer home in an effort to keep his wife off the streets. It was in vain.

One Saturday night, in her usual inebriated state, she was captured in a Salvation Army 'Drunks Raid' and taken by the Slum Officers arm in arm, to an evangelistic meeting in the hall. Mrs. Potts, her clothes filthy from lying in the street, was too drunk really to take in what was going on. But, before leaving her at her own front door, the officers had put in her pocket a copy of *The War Cry* and an invitation to come to the Sunday night meeting at the Slum Post.

When an unusually clean, sober, but uncertain Mrs. Potts put in an appearance at the meeting the next night, the Slum Officer gave her a warm welcome and a friendly handshake. The woman, used to cuffs and curses, was deeply touched by the simple kindliness of the officer and began to relax and enjoy herself, attending for several weeks before realising that God was asking her to do something more.

She knelt at the Mercy Seat one Sunday evening, to show her repentance and her desire to start afresh. It was a miracle, and certainly her family found it hard to believe it would last. They had been so ashamed of her previous exploits and attempts to leave the drink alone, that they had little faith in this new development.

They were wrong — and the testimony of all who knew Mrs. Potts agreed — she had obviously received pardon and had completely left her old way of life. She might bear the scars of those street fights on her body still — but her smile was different.

Sometimes depressed and tired by the demands of her new calling, especially the visiting, Martha comforted herself with the memory of Mrs. Potts' conversion. Without the determination of those two Slum Officers, she might still have been fighting her street battles. Martha knew she must press on. Perhaps behind one of the doors on which she was knocking, would be another hidden jewel like Mrs. Potts.

Martha found herself called upon more and more to sit with elderly and sick people at short notice, so it was her custom always to carry with her a small folding chair. She never knew when she might have to sit up all night with an extremely sick person. Often it was not just sitting, it was nursing and caring for them physically and helping to keep the sickroom clean — usually in dreadful conditions with little light and air, and plenty of dirt, damp and draughts. Scrubbing out sickrooms was a regular chore done by Slum Officers, for in the late thirties home helps hadn't been thought of, and district nurses had enough work to do. 'Meals on wheels' also were a thing of the future, and the hot dinners cooked and distributed by the Army were pioneers of later welfare work.

It was in Bristol that Martha found one aspect of her college training coming into its own — laying out the dead. It strikes the modern, non-medical person as slightly 'morbid' perhaps. But many of the poorer people who could not afford proper medical care, and often could not pay for funerals, called upon the Army's help.

Martha had learnt all about the subject at college, but her first few experiences 'for real' were quite traumatic. She had visited one old lady regularly and knew that her struggle with the ghastly disease which was ravaging her body was nearly over. Her condition was rapidly deteriorating and Martha sat with her one night on her little folding chair, trying to give her what succour she could in appalling circumstances of little light or ventilation and no heating. For Martha it was a first experience of someone dying, and she was frightened. When she was certain that the woman was dead she took great pains to prepare the body properly for burial though in the poor light and the stench it was terribly difficult. What troubled her most of all was the bed. It was filthy and not only useless, but also a dangerous source of infection. Yet if she managed somehow to destroy the bed where would the body lie until the undertaker came? Recalling her college lectures she remembered that when no furniture provided a suitable surface, a door might be used. Calling on a neighbour to help they removed a door from its hinges for the body to lie on, and then burnt the bed.

In January 1936 word came that Captain Stewart was to leave Bedminster and a new Commanding Officer would be arriving. Her name was Adjutant Ada Aldred.

Martha said goodbye to May Stewart with real sorrow for she had fully appreciated her leadership and understanding.

Adjutant Aldred's conviction was that at all costs nothing should distract them from upholding the programme laid down in their training for Slum work. The weekday routine was kept rigidly to schedule with both officers uniformed and ready to go out on the district by 10.00 a.m. This might mean that her Lieutenant had been doing her share of the cleaning, and washing and ironing, as well as fulfilling her personal and devotional requirements, from quite an early hour. But even so, Aldred expected no unnecessary creases in the large aprons they used, and did not want to see dust and dirt where they shouldn't be. There was no getting away from it, she was fussy, and the slightest crumple in Martha's laundering meant 'back to the ironing board, Field'.

In fact compared with Aldred's strictness and dignified manner, Captain Stewart's firmness appeared almost lax! But, for all her sternness Adjutant Aldred gave her Lieutenant good training—and she was always scrupulously fair.

Martha's folding chair was put to good use, on many a night of sick-nursing, particularly as the grim shadows of Nazism lengthened across Europe, culminating in the Second World War. The work of the Salvation Army officers became increasingly essential and important.

But before the outbreak of war, Martha once again was thrown into a demanding yet rewarding stint on the hopfields. It was Worcestershire this time and even harder work than in Kent, with many neglected children to tend.

One young mother brought her ten-month-old to the 'crèche' leaving a pack of thick sandwiches for his lunch and a pint of milk in a lemonade bottle with the finger top of an old glove tied on with a dirty piece of cotton to act as a teat.

Martha's tasks included collecting wood, filling the field boiler, heating the water for washing and tea-making, and caring for physical needs at the First Aid post. There was also the challenge of the gospel presented in conversation, testimony, singing and preaching; all combined to make the three weeks a memorable experience in the midst of beautiful, fruitful countryside.

Martha and her fellow officers found the going extra tough in those weeks, especially as the lady of the farm house, thought that such new-fangled notions as putting the clocks forward for British Summer Time were not for her. Her 'guests' never knew whether they were on time, an hour ahead, or an hour behind! You just had to laugh — it was no good getting agitated about it.

Indeed Slum work, with all its pressures, often brought moments of high comedy when release from tension came in laughter, as well as moments of deepest tragedy, when tears alone brought relief to the burdened spirit. Martha came to know both.

Now and then some unexpected, heartwarming event lit up the mundane, like the sun breaking through clouds, confirming God's hand upon her life. So it was the night Martha was lost in the fog in Bristol. Like so many places not far from the sea and with industrial fumes from factory chimneys Bristol had frequent fogs, especially in winter.

On Christmas Eve, 1938, Captain Martha Field — she had been made Captain in May — was walking a little wearily home to the quarters from pub-booming in the city centre. Her stock of papers had almost gone, as the pubs had been full. The fog, clammy and cold, caught at her throat. It swirled around the street lamps, though away from the city centre these were few and far between. The darkness seemed impenetrable and the mournful sound of foghorns floating up from the River Avon added to her feeling of isolation.

How long it took her to discover she was really lost, she could not say, but so thick was the fog and darkness that she lost her bearings completely. She stopped, hoping that by slowly turning round on the spot, a familiar shape or sign would be visible. All she could see was a faint light somewhere in the distance.

Huddling into her uniform coat in an effort to keep out the cold, Martha walked carefully along the pavement until she could see the light's source. It was a small cottage. Relieved to have found someone who might be able to help her, she knocked at the front door. It was opened almost immediately by a young woman, who at the sight of Martha burst into tears.

'Come in, oh come in,' she sobbed.

'What is it, dear?' Martha asked, startled but anxious to help, as the woman continued to sob as if her heart was breaking, unable to speak for tears.

Martha sat her down and looked around for some means of distracting or comforting her. On the plain kitchen dresser were five small stockings, bulging with bon-bons and small packets and sprigs of holly.

'My! Those look lovely, sure they do,' she said. 'Five little people are going to have a wonderful surprise tomorrow.'

'But I haven't got five now,' the woman wailed. She led Martha to the corner of the living-room. Lying on a bed was the body of a small child. Martha put her arm round the distraught mother and led her back to her seat, then began to look for some way to prepare a hot drink. The cupboard was almost bare, there was no sign of any Christmas fare for the next day. Furthermore Martha was distressed to discover that the husband was ill in bed upstairs, and the other four children asleep and unaware of the tragedy that had overtaken the family.

Martha felt sure that God had led her to this home in the fog for a purpose. She reassured the mother promising to return as soon as possible with food from the Slum Post.

On such occasions, Martha drew on the special sum of money given by the Army to the Slum Officers for needy cases. To supplement this the work also depended upon the gifts of local people, national charities and the Goodwill League newly founded by Hugh Redwood. At Christmas many friends of the Army gave toys for distribution to poor families. But all the year round there was a steady flow: gifts of money to buy food or small luxuries; secondhand clothes for needy children; stocks of food or drugs for the elderly and needy often given by food or drug manufacturers. During and after the war when coal was scarce, it was often the Army's task to distribute special stocks to the elderly. In fact, many items which today's National Health Service and Welfare State provide were not then to be had unless donated. The Slum Officers were often a life-line to people in direct need.

In those days tuberculosis was a common and terrible scourge, and The Salvation Army tried to do what it could to help fight the misery. Special free milk supplies were available for poor families. Martha was instructed how to arrange with the milkman to deliver the vital pints to the right homes, and see that the bill went to the Slum Post. It was heartbreaking for her, only eighteen months out of college, to have to nurse one family where not only the father but two teenage girls died within the space of a year of the dread complaint.

Supplying blankets during the winter months was another regular service. Needy families borrowed the blankets at the end of October, returning them at the end of March, unless the recipient was incurably ill and needed the extra warmth. All blankets on their return were fumigated, then stored until the next October.

Again, the many social services which are offered today by different organisations and relief agencies — the WVS, Help the Aged, Shelter, for instance — were handled then by the Army's Slum Officers. Problems of battered wives, battered babies, broken homes — matters which are now considered the province of the health visitor or children's officer — are problems long known and dealt with by Salvation Army officers.

It was seeing the tremendous demands made of 'The Slums' (as the officers were often called) that inspired Hugh Redwood to suggest the setting up of the Goodwill League. It is hard to estimate the immense contribution made to the cause of The Salvation Army, and its slum and goodwill work in particular, through his inspired idea.

From his first contact with 'The Slums' during the Thames flood disaster in 1928, Hugh Redwood gave unstintingly of his time and talents and money to forward the Army's goodwill work. His journalistic gifts used in *God in the Slums* and *God in the Shadows*, brought many women into training for officership and service, as Martha herself and many of her friends were able to testify. More than that, Hugh Redwood was always doing the unexpected good deed for this hardpressed band, to lighten their burden amongst the needy and improve the conditions under which they were living and working. Stories of his generosity and humour abound, his thoughtfulness and sympathy, and his willingness to take his jacket off and get his own hands dirty, alongside the Army officers.

Perhaps it was fitting that Martha should meet him first

in Bristol, for from the age of six, the city had been his home. Who better could give a guided tour of the city? He had grown up, been educated and started his newspaper career there. Captain Field and her colleague found themselves ushered into a taxi — a luxury they could never afford — and whisked round the city, seeing Hugh Redwood's home, his school, his church and even the place where he met his first girl friend! Bristol came to have quite a new significance for Martha after that, and Hugh Redwood's cheerful bespectacled face and plump figure was a welcome and regular sight at Wilway Street. If he came to Bristol he stayed not at the best hotels, but with 'The Slums'.

Did Martha ever share her experience in the Bristol fog with him? She might have discovered he too had had a meaningful encounter on Durdham Down in a thick fog . . . and one that was to remain with him for life. As a boy he had explored every inch of the Down — 'a glorious stretch of common land' as he called it, not two miles from the city's centre. Indeed he knew it so well that even in the dark or thick fog he could 'navigate' his way across it without any difficulty. 'I would set myself a definite objective, the lamp with a red glass to it, for instance, which marked, on the opposite side of the Down, the road which one took to the Folly. From the moment I set foot on the grass, I had no light at all by which to take bearings. I knew the distance and general direction, and I knew the feel of the ground beneath me. But there was something else, which I cannot define. I focused my thoughts on that one lamp, and it was almost as if they found their way to it and sent back a beam for me to follow, so that presently, out of the murk, I would see the red light straight before me.'

When much later God touched Hugh Redwood's life he returned to that earlier experience and repeated the questions he asked then: 'Can we get guidance of other kinds in similar fashion? In spiritual darkness or fog can we so focus our minds on one great Objective as to establish a communion which will, so to speak "bring us on beam"?' He believed the answer was yes. 'Now for the first time I deliberately trusted myself to it. I was learning how to pray: I endeavoured to stay my mind upon God and put aside every reservation. I said in effect "Lead Thou me on. I will not ask to see the distant scene, but when it comes to the next step, dear Lord, take charge of my feet." I have made that my prayer ever since, and I have no doubt at all that God has guided me in answer to it.'

Hugh Redwood's kindness meant a lot to the two Bristol Slum Officers, and the support of local friends counted for a great deal also. One family, well-known in Bedminster, were always ready to help anyone.

4

Wartime Manchester and Disaster

'They're here! They're here!' shrieked Mrs. Jones in the middle of the Home League meeting. Struggling to her feet, she clutched her vast black handbag to her equally vast black satin bust. The drone of engines overhead meant only one thing to her — German planes on a bombing raid.

'Now, dearie! To be sure they're ours,' Martha said soothingly. 'There's been no air raid warning. Sit ye down.'

'Oh thank God they're not real ones then,' Bertha Jones gasped, subsiding and relaxing her grip on her bag.

Comforting the frightened and guiding them down to safety in the shelters during bombing raids became almost a nightly routine for Martha when she was sent, with Major Aldred, to the Slum Post in Gibson Street, Ardwick, south-west of Manchester.

Keeping everyone cheerful once they were in the shelters was also part of their demanding task. Yet people like Bertha Jones helped; for once her fears were dispelled she could soon brighten any group with a song or two. Like so many other wives and mothers she had seen her menfolk go off to fight, and was proud of them. With four sons in the Royal Navy her favourite tune was 'Sons of the Sea. All British born' sung with great gusto especially when she was slightly tipsy.

Before Martha and Major Aldred had left Bedminster in May 1940, the grim realities of war had begun to make themselves felt. Gasmasks, rationing, black-out, air raid warnings, bomb craters and queues became common sights as did the parties of solemn-faced, often tearful, children with their small suitcases, and labels, waving goodbye to parents as evacuation trains took them to safety. The city centre of Bristol itself suffered from air attacks; but then so did Manchester, where the two women were appointed. They took up their duties without a break.

The salt tang of sea air was not to be found as easily in Ardwick as in Bristol. The grimy waters of the Manchester Ship Canal, the Irwell or the Mersey could represent at least a tenuous link with Liverpool Bay and the Irish Sea. Wartime restrictions on travel, however, prevented Martha from taking the boat home to Belfast from Liverpool, and her three weeks yearly furlough had to be spent in England.

The narrow terraced streets of back-to-back houses, the tall black smoking factory and mill chimneys blotting out the sky with their soot, the pubs and the pawn-shops on every corner all bore a striking resemblance to the 'Coronation Street' of later TV fame.

Yet the tough, cheerful Mancunians, in the midst of wartime privations and bombing raids, impressed Martha as they came up smiling from the shelters after each night of blitz. She and Major Aldred were in the thick of it almost as soon as they arrived. For many, many nights the planes continued their lethal attacks and they and their fellow officers from other corps and divisional headquarters were out helping alongside the hard-pressed emergency services. Guiding distressed families to safety, caring for mothers with babes-in-arms, shepherding the very young and the very old down the steps of the shelters or just chatting, encouraging or joking to comfort those who were obviously frightened—it was all in a night's work. Then there were shelter teas when the Army would provide refreshments, and impromptu children's meetings down in the shelter to keep the little ones' minds off the danger overhead.

On really bad nights they were usually on call to give support to the fire, ambulance and police during the bombing raids. Rolling out the tea urn reminded Martha of her happy days on the hopfields, though the circumstances were sadly different. No tangy smell of hops or woodsmoke here, but the scorched, burnt-rubber smell of buildings fired by incendiaries, the charred embers and the terrible sight of injured and dead.

In the thick of that first winter's holocaust, the cold and the fog took their toll of Ada Aldred's health. A chest condition aggravated by exhaustion, grime and smog, led the Army to move her back to the south of England in January 1941. It was a shock to Martha for they had been at Ardwick together for such a short time. What would happen to her, she wondered. Would she have a new C.O. or be moved elsewhere?

Her love for the people at Ardwick was to be a deciding factor, for Lt.-Colonel Edith Wootton, the Slum and Goodwill Secretary at headquarters, met Martha in Liverpool and heard her speak of her work. Instead of moving Martha, as had originally been planned, she wrote:

> 'I have pleasure in appointing you in charge of the Ardwick Post.
>
> 'Having seen for myself how you have put your heart and soul into your work and how God has honoured you I feel that such an opportunity is due to you . . . I have prayed much about this—I can see you now at the supper table a few weeks ago telling your stories and I

know that the same spirit that animated you then will help you through and keep you a servant of all for your Master's sake.

'I am sending you a Lieutenant from Paddington Goodwill Centre . . .'

Not only Lieutenant Gray came, but also Lieutenant Winnie Bewick, straight from the training college, as Assistant Officer. The team of three was not to be together for long, for the pressure of work meant Gray had to be put in charge at another post. But while they were together they shared in fellowship and some funny moments which lightened the heavy schedule.

Winnie Bewick had been a midwife before entering the training college. She enjoyed helping the Mums with their new-born babies. Martha had discovered her own special gift for sick nursing and caring for the dying. It became quite a joke — that with one helping to bring people into the world and the other helping to care for those who were leaving it, Gray had to make do with what was left in between.

Lieutenant Winnie Bewick was to prove a tower of strength to her C.O. She was the first of two large-framed, large-hearted Assistant Officers for whom Martha was particularly to thank God. As a widow of twenty-six in Nottingham, where she was nursing, she had responded to the call to serve God through the Army. Home was actually in Sunderland where she had been brought up a Primitive Methodist. One Sunday morning in William Booth's native city, she followed the Salvation Army band, attracted like Martha by the music, and entered the Memorial Halls, where she found challenge and a call to Christian service such as she had never heard before. Believing she was too old for training, she nonetheless offered herself for Slum and Goodwill work, and was accepted. After her nine months' training, Ardwick and Captain Martha Field were her first experience of Slum work.

It was a tough start and weaker souls than Winnie, would have wilted and fallen by the wayside in the first three months. The blitz was appalling — a nightly occurrence — laying heavier than usual burdens on the Slum Officers. Meanwhile Martha, in charge for the first time, was taking her duties towards her new assistant officer very seriously. She was not going to lower standards just because there was a war on. In spite of all kinds of interruptions and inconveniences, the routine of the Post was upheld. Early rising — even if they had been out late the night before — the meticulous cleaning of quarters, and then out on the district at 10.00 a.m. There was always something to be doing, and yet time must also be set aside for quiet and prayer and Bible reading.

If her Captains had seemed strict with Martha, Captain Field appeared just as strict to Lieutenant Bewick. Yet as before, respect and affection grew out of what started as a working relationship. Each recognised in the other a disciplined person, and Captain Field never asked her 'Leff' to do anything she was not prepared to do herself. They also shared a deep sense of humour that helped to oil the wheels on many occasions.

Not surprisingly the dreadful battering of disturbed nights began to tire the two women. They never refused a call for assistance. It became the Chief Fire Officer's habit to ring Captain Field and her assistant first before contacting other centres for voluntary help.

The women usually manned the portable tea urn or gave First Aid to any injured among the rescue workers. Often in great danger themselves, it was a miracle that they escaped unscathed. On more than one occasion they were asked to withdraw to safety, but refused. On one night when the city centre suffered some of its worst bombing, the mobile canteen was almost destroyed and the Divisional Officer had a lucky escape. The Chief Fire Officer again suggested that the women withdraw but, inspired by the dedication of others in the face of danger, they would not retreat.

On a night that Martha was never to forget, the nearby Royal Artillery Barracks received a direct hit, and many young men and recruits were killed or buried in the rubble. The rescue operation went on, night and day, with the Army giving its assistance with tea and First Aid all that time. A few nights later the Ardwick Hippodrome was destroyed and warehouses in the city centre.

That was an incredible sight. The warehouses in Portland Street near Piccadilly Square, Manchester, were ablaze from end to end. The situation became exceedingly dangerous and having tried once to get the women to withdraw, a slightly bizarre incident managed to do what the Fire Officer's pleas could not. Out of one of the huge cavernous warehouses, now well alight, came a large black cat with one kitten in its mouth. It laid this gently at the feet of the rescue workers and disappeared into the smoke once again, returning four times with a kitten until the family of five were safe.

The firemen and exhausted rescuers stood around amazed at this display of courage and tenacity. 'Right, Captain,' the Fire Officer said. 'I'm sure you want a cat down at Ardwick. Now's your chance. How about finding a box or basket or something and taking this little lot home?'

Despite the chaos Captain managed to find a basket, and a lift to Ardwick for the six heroes was commandeered, Martha flagging down a slightly bemused driver who agreed, in the face of her determination, to take them all out to the Slum Post.

Cats were by no means the only bomb victims. Major Algernon Fensom the officer from Manchester Temple

Corps and his family were made homeless, escaping injury in a truly incredible way. Mrs. Fensom and their small son were out when a bomb went through the centre of their home — the part which Mrs. Fensom had always considered the safest. The adjoining citadel was untouched, but the Fensoms lost everything.

Within twenty minutes of the bomb falling, a car with Captain Field and Lieutenant Bewick arrived to take the slightly dazed family to the Slum Post, where, without a word being said, it was assumed that the family would live. For a month Gibson Street's converted pub was the Fensom's home, until new quarters could be found for them.

Often, Major Fensom saw distressed people, who had lost everything in an air raid, come to the Post for second-hand clothes and find Martha a source of cheerfulness. Their fitting out was used as a chance to forget their problems for a moment in a good laugh. This happened to Fensom himself on the night he lost his home. The family long remembered the hilarious 'dressing-up' session which ended with father conducting a Salvation Army meeting in plus fours!

But Martha's humour knew its limits. If petty bureaucracy stood in her way she drew the line. When a City Councillor was being tightfisted over the distribution of food parcels from Canada, Martha dispensed with frivolities. Her determined plea and her accurate assessment of need in her district and the exact number in each home or family that she was in touch with, so impressed the Council that she achieved the much-needed parcels with no further trouble.

Yet all this extra work had somehow to fit in with the weekly meetings and other claims at the Slum Post. There was a fairly full programme for old and young to be kept going despite everything. Amidst the general wartime tensions it was often the young people who provided the brightest moments. Certainly the Children's Clubs, held twice weekly, were a source of encouragement. The lads in particular were always ready to lend a hand to help Captain and 'Leff' and they never took advantage of the two women. Vandalism in the Army Hall and property was unheard of. Even though most of the sixteen boys between the ages of eleven and fourteen came from difficult homes, the two officers managed to cope with them. Usually the clubs provided facilities for games — such as billiards and draughts and bagatelle — then refreshments for which a small charge was made. A short service completed the session.

They soon found it helped to give the worst-behaved boys some responsibility and, if the meetings were interrupted by the sound of an air raid warning, it was often these boys who proved the most eager to guide the elderly or blind who needed assistance down to the shelter, or to comfort the younger children who were scared.

The frantic pace at which they had been living, with demands being made on them day and night brought both women to a low ebb. Suddenly Martha, without any warning collapsed. She had driven herself literally to a standstill.

She had been visiting a mother, recently widowed, and had taken some warm clothing for the small boy. About to leave, Martha found she had difficulty in standing. Somehow she managed to get back to the quarters and the doctor was called. He was an old friend and said solemnly as he entered the bedroom to examine her, 'So the Captain has fallen in the battle!' He prescribed a month's rest at a local sanatorium — confirming Martha's worst fears — that she might have caught a T.B. germ — or worse.

She confessed her fears to her Divisional Commander, who agreed that he would get the doctor's consent to send her away completely. Still unable to travel to Belfast for a rest at home, it was to Major Aldred that she went for three months' sick furlough at the Salvation Army's Rest Home, Herne Bay, Kent.

Major Aldred was horrified to see, instead of the smiling, bonny Lieutenant she remembered, a haggard, pale figure, weak from overwork and lack of proper food and sleep. Secretly she thought that Martha had come there to die . . . but the devoted care she and the staff gave her, changed all that.

Martha was grateful to her ex-C.O. for her care and loving encouragement, for she needed it. Her worries about not coming up to expectations were never far away, and this collapse revived them. Her first efforts at being 'in charge' had ended in her coming to grief healthwise. Would she be relieved of her duties at Ardwick? Who would take charge if that happened? The Salvation Army had the wisdom to set her mind at rest with an assurance that she was still needed. More aware of her limitations than before, Martha returned to the Ardwick Post in February 1944 and never looked back.

5

Ardwick and Apple Charlotte

'Now, Bewick, what have you been up to?' Captain Field said sternly as she came in from visiting. 'It's to Granny Flannigan's I've been and she says to me, "Now, Captain, don't let that big one come here any more. It's an old horse she thinks she's washing — not a delicate old lady!" '

The 'big one' was, of course, Lieutenant Winnie Bewick, and Granny Flannigan was just one of the many 'characters' who lived near the Ardwick Slum Post. As soon as Winnie had arrived at Ardwick, Martha had asked her to visit Granny and 'do' for her. This Winnie had done, washing Granny with all the cheerful vigour of a newly-commissioned Slum Officer out to save the world. And here was her first C.O. reporting a complaint already. Winnie looked down at her hands ruefully. They were still swollen and pink from the hard work she had put in with the scrubbing brush as well as soap and flannel. Had it all been wasted effort? Was she really suited to this work?

She looked up miserably and caught sight of a twinkle in Martha's eye. 'Aw, don't despair, Lieutenant,' she said consolingly. 'Granny's a great soul, and doesn't hold it against you. She does appreciate it, really she does. . .'

'Her cat doesn't, though,' Winnie said, smiling with relief. 'He came in today, took one look at my clean floor and stalked out. "'E reckons 'e's in the wrong 'ouse," Granny says, "'e's never seen pattern on lino before!"'

Captain and Lieutenant laughed together, though their amusement soon gave way to prayer for Granny Flannigan, who suffered terribly with legs ulcerated down to the bone.

If Winnie felt despondent at times about her progress as a Slum Officer her visits to Mrs. Nolan made a big difference. She was a regular attender at the Salvation Army meetings, and was grateful for the help of the officers in her home. Amidst all the muck and soot from the factory chimneys, she kept her little house clean and neat. It was a pleasure to see it. Then Mrs. Nolan herself was a tonic. She loved singing hymns and choruses with her visitors, and often, if Winnie felt tired and dispirited about the toughness of the work, a chat to Mrs. Nolan about God's love and goodness helped to revitalise her. Perhaps it was that they loved the same songs, but Winnie always felt spurred on after visiting her.

Mrs. Maddox came to the meetings also; always neatly dressed in hat and coat. When the officers went to her home, they were welcomed into her tiny stone-flagged front room where she was sitting by the fireplace with a little rag mat at her feet. There was a scullery behind but visitors never got beyond that front room. It might have been a desire for privacy or pride, for Mrs. Maddox had known better days. Her husband, they were told, had been next in line for Lord Mayor at one time. But now his widow lived with one son in sadly reduced circumstances. How reduced only became apparent when she was taken seriously ill.

When the neighbours told Martha, she and Winnie hurried round to see what help they could give. In response to their knock, the door was opened by the son, whom they scarcely ever saw. Grimfaced and unwelcoming, he indicated surlily that his mother was upstairs. Martha asked if they could go up, and for the first time they were allowed to enter the scullery to get to the staircase. They were appalled at what they found. The scullery was littered from floor to ceiling with piles upon piles of newspapers and the unmistakable signs of rat-infestation. Pushing their way through the accumulated mounds of filth they reached the dark narrow uncarpeted stairs. Upstairs was no better. The rats were up there, too, for the dirt and squalor got worse. The floors were bare, as were the windows, and the glass panes had not been cleaned for years. The light could barely filter through into the room, and after some difficulty they found Mrs. Maddox in bed in the gloom.

Martha talked gently to the pathetically frail figure huddled in the bed while Winnie took stock of the room. One corner appeared to have been partitioned off she assumed for the son to use as a den with lace curtains, black as black. She stepped closer. It wasn't black lace at all. It was the thickest, sootiest cobwebs she had ever seen, dangling from ceiling, walls and furniture. When Martha called her to the bedside it was no surprise to see the bed was in the same state as the rest of the house. The two women decided on a plan of campaign.

First Mrs. Maddox must be persuaded to have a blanket bath and a change of night attire. Her emaciated body was all curled up in the squalid bedclothes. Talking quietly to her, they began to remove the tattered blankets, but she seemed strangely reluctant to let them carry out their wishes. Neither of them could understand why, until they came to lift her. Clenched between her knees was an old purse stuffed with what looked like crumpled newspaper. It was dirty pound notes, hidden because her son took every penny she had for drink, denying his mother any of the decencies of life. Her claw-like hands clutched at the purse, and Martha had to reassure her gently that they would not tell her son of this pathetic attempt to prevent him stealing what was rightly hers.

Poor Mrs. Maddox! Martha thought as she hastened off to fetch clean bedclothes and a nightdress.

The two women tackled the filthy room as well, glad to knock down and destroy the foul cobwebs and throw away the piles of festering rubbish and newspapers, scouring the floor thoroughly with disinfectant afterwards until their hands were swollen and stinging from scrubbing. Mrs. Maddox's doctor was overjoyed and amazed. He had longed to see the place cleaned up, but had not had the courage to ask anyone to tackle such filth.

Ardwick certainly provided plenty of 'special cases', as Martha and Winnie termed them. These people endeared themselves to Martha for their grit and humour often in the face of ghastly circumstances. Many had known a better standard of living, yet faced misfortunes without complaint, hiding their troubles if they felt there were others worse off than themselves. Martha and Winnie were often told about needy people but sometimes they came to the Home League meetings at the post.

Among the former was Blind Billy whom they met through one of the women attending the Home League. They paid him a visit, and found a tragic situation. Living entirely alone in the downstairs room of a decrepit stone-flagged little terraced house, he could scarcely walk and had got himself into a shocking state. Everything that he needed for daily life was stowed in one dilapidated arm-chair near the fireplace where he sat all day long. In his blindness he wanted to know exactly where his baccy, his pipe, his toothbrush and his soap and flannel were, and to prevent his food being over-run by mice. In that chair his food and his toilet articles and his pipe and matches were all shoved higgledy-piggledy.

In one corner of the room stood a sagging bedstead, and

across the front of the fireplace in which he somehow managed to light a fire and cook his food, was a heavy marble slab which had fallen from the broken mantelpiece.

Martha and Winnie could not lift it and called on the help of Salvationist Bandsmen from nearby Higher Openshaw to help clear out the room in readiness for some better furniture. A decent bed was provided by the Women's Social Work with linen and blankets. And a new set of shelves were placed beside his cleaned and mended armchair.

As they continued to visit Billy they learnt more of his sad story. His blindness was not congenital, but the result of a stupid and dangerous prank at work. One of the lads had thrown a rag soaked in naphtha at someone else who ducked; Billy caught it full in the face. Not realising what it was he clutched it instead of knocking the cloth away. His eyes were burned and his sight was ruined. Later he took to drink and was knocked down by a tram in the centre of Manchester. His broken legs were set so badly that he could barely hobble about. He'd tried since then to cut down on drinking, and in this the two Salvation Army officers were happy to help and encourage him.

The chief problem came when they considered moving Billy to a better house. The condition of the other, plus the ever-present mice population, forced this upon them, and the only suitable place they could find was situated between two pubs! It looked like putting temptation right under his nose, but there was no alternative.

Word soon got around that Billy was being moved to a new home, and would be needing a few items of furniture to stock it. It was heartwarming to see neighbours rallying round and despite wartime shortages, donating a kitchen chair, a table, a lamp or a few pieces of cutlery and crockery. The move took place with the help of Salvation Army friends and Billy settled in to his new home amazingly quickly. With regular visits from the two officers, who collected his pension and his groceries and kept his place clean, he seemed to make great strides and improved in every way. He mastered the boiler in the back scullery of the new place remarkably well and learnt to fill and light it, then ladle out enough to have a wash. But for a bath, one of the men Salvationists would take him down to the public baths, and help him to have a proper shave. If Hugh Redwood was staying in Ardwick, as he did on one or two occasions while Martha was there — this was just the sort of job he loved doing.

Alcohol was a problem to many families around the centre. A knock at the main door of the Slum Post at midnight brought Martha down. A young girl in some distress asked if the Salvation Army officers could come please, her father was dying. Bewick accompanying her, Martha set off to find the house. The wife was in an even more distressed state than her daughter and led the two women upstairs where flat on his back in bed was her husband, fully dressed with his cap on and a red and white spotted scarf still round his neck.

Martha immediately tried to loosen his scarf and take off his cap. As she bent over to see what First Aid could be given him she was sure she could smell alcohol.

'Are you sure he's not been drinking, then?' she asked his wife as she continued to inspect the unconscious man for any signs of injury.

'Oh no! He's not had a drink all day, miss. I'm sure that he's not,' the woman adamantly replied.

There was nothing for it but to test to see if he was unconscious or just asleep. Martha took a matchstick and tried to fold back his eyelids. The response was immediate. The 'corpse' jumped up out of the bed giving Martha a terrible smack on the face as it did so. Martha and Winnie made their way wearily home once more.

The next morning the husband, looking slightly embarrassed and ill at ease, arrived very early at the quarters. He wanted to apologise for the whole incident. He had been drunk and he had also been under the impression that it was his Missis who had received the smack in the face, not the Salvation Army officer. He was sorry to have put them to such trouble.

Another knock at the Slum Post door late on a Saturday night became a regular routine, and the 'temporary' residents for the night were the Lockett family. When Mr. Lockett got drunk, as he invariably did at weekends, he would knock his wife about and go for the children. So not only Mrs. Lockett but all the ten Lockett children took refuge with the Army. Martha and Winnie would put them to sleep on the forms in the hall, with what clothes and pillows could be mustered to make them comfortable. It was a pathetic sight and one which touched Martha deeply, for it seemed so wrong that the little ones should have to suffer this insecurity.

Like Mrs. Maddox's son, some children Martha met did not touch her heart. She found their lack of love and loyalty for their parents staggering. The neighbours who asked them to visit one neglected old man assumed he had no family to care for him because on more than one occasion he had been seen in the street, dirty and unshaven with his clothing undone. They were wrong.

When Martha and Winnie first called on him he was in a bed that was alive with bedbugs. Someone had tried to kill them and there were splotches of blood and squashed corpses all over the place. So neglected had he become that he and his bedclothes were lifting with the great slow-moving insects.

Fighting down their distaste the two women set about cleaning him up. A visit to the public baths was arranged while they burnt his bed and bedding. Then another bed and clean linen was found from the Army. They left him more comfortable than he had been for months, possibly years, with a promise of weekly visits to keep an eye on him. The visits seemed to enliven him. Having been a Methodist all his life, he was never happier than when the Captain or Lieutenant sang a hymn or two to him, while they were working, or sat down to pray or read the Bible.

They tried to keep an eye on his appearance, too, and saw that he was shaved regularly. Occasionally they nagged him to buy some small necessity but he seemed very reluctant. He wasn't without money but he appeared very tightfisted, never paying a halfpenny when a farthing would do.

One afternoon, after visiting 'Buggy Billy' as they called him affectionately to differentiate him from Blind Billy, Martha arrived back at the quarters steaming with indignation.

'Bewick, you'll not believe it. Buggy Billy has got a family after all — a married daughter what is more, living not far away, in a posh house, with no children and no worries. She's just been to see her father this week, Mrs. Hardcastle says. And she comes just for his money about once a quarter. Not to see if her father's doing all right — oh no — just to clean him out of his cash. I don't believe she puts a foot beyond that front room for she'd not have left him in that state we found him in, would she? If we hadn't gone in and done for him where would he have been?'

So strongly did Martha feel that the daughter had a responsibility towards her own father, that she took the unusual step of writing to her. She explained that her concern was for her father's welfare and asked if it was right that the neighbours had had to call in The Salvation Army to keep him clean and decent when he had a daughter not far away. If she paid a visit once a quarter to take his money, could she not take him home with her — or see that he was properly cared for?

It was Winnie's turn to visit Buggy Billy the next week. She found the house empty. Any high hopes that the daughter had opened her home to her father were soon dashed when the neighbours told her he had been put in the Workhouse at Withington. Martha and Winnie continued to visit him there regularly and were relieved to see that he was not unduly bothered by the move and settled down happily enough.

By comparison with Buggy Billy, Billy Kemp was well able to take care of himself even though he was blind. It was his wife's need that first brought Martha into contact with him for Annie Kemp was very ill and needed special nursing. The neighbours were good to the Kemps, so there was not the need for 'home helping' in the usual way, but Martha would sit up with Annie. In fact the night she died Martha had sat with her until 1 a.m., when a neighbour had come in to let her go back to the quarters to get some sleep. A call at the door in the early hours brought Martha quickly out of bed. She was a light sleeper and it took very little to wake her. Annie had finally passed away — would Captain come? Hastily washing her face and tidying her uniform, Martha collected together her bag and apron before going to the Kemps. With the help of the neighbour they began to lay out the body. Billy Kemp, obviously just up from his bed, with his hair tousled and dressing-gown on, came into the bedroom as they were finishing.

'Are you all right, Billy?' Martha asked anxiously.

'Well, Captain,' he said, running his hand through his hair. 'It's like this. I can't live here by myself now Annie's gone, can I? I was wonderin' — have you ever thought of getting married?'

Billy was not deterred by Martha's lack of interest. If Captain wouldn't have him, then somebody else would. For all his blindness he knew what he wanted, and could make sure he got it. They were not surprised when, before six months had past, he had married again. His new wife was an old lady who ran a little corner shop that sold sweets, baccy, drinks and newspapers, and all sorts of other small items. Martha and Winnie couldn't help smiling at the thought of him having all his home comforts — on the house!

Martha was convinced that the wartime insecurities made people more spiritually aware during the time they were in Ardwick. Nearly everyone she visited appreciated the time when she opened her Bible or knelt to pray, and all would join in a bit of hymn or chorus singing. Often the person she was visiting would be on their knees as soon as they saw the Captain move to leave.

Prayer for Martha was as natural as breathing anyway. And she believed in asking God's help for the ordinary day-to-day matters as well as the bigger things like 'peace in our time'. She would bring to God the simple anxieties of the housewife or mother she was visiting; the need for healing for a sick child; the relief from pain for an old man stricken with rheumatism; or just the need for a loaf of bread or a shilling for the meter. Nothing was too small or too big. And for one person Martha's prayer was a turning point.

Lottie was a great local character, very kind-hearted and full of generosity and good humour. She cleaned the local pub The Rose and Crown, and was fond of her drink. So fond, that when pay day came each week, she had subbed all her wages 'on the slate' and rarely had anything left to take home. Very popular with the other 'shawlies' who went to the pub, when the drink was in her, her tongue could get carried away. One evening, for instance, she gaily informed her mates: 'When my ole man snuffs it, dearies, I'll treat you all!'

Which wouldn't have struck anyone as significant except that, unfortunately for Lottie, during the following week her husband did indeed 'snuff it'. She was shattered — for they had been happy together and she was genuinely fond of him. Of course, she had been only joking when she had made her foolish offer but it sat heavily on her conscience. She was sure God had taken her 'ole man' as a punishment for her irreverent treatment of the subject of death. Not one for religion of any sort, she had noticed a Salvation Army officer passing the pub and decided to ask for some help.

In the gloom of a dark November afternoon Martha was suddenly stopped in her tracks by two hands laid on her shoulders from behind. Turning around she saw an older woman, tears streaming down her chubby cheeks.

'Will you come home with me, luv?' the woman asked brokenly. 'I want you to pray for me.'

They were soon in the tiny front room of Lottie's house and the whole story came pouring out . . . 'And I want you to please pray to God to forgive me for what I said about Jack. I never meant it.' Tears stopped Lottie again. 'I really miss him awful. Do you think God can heal my broken heart?'

Martha and Lottie knelt on the rag rug in front of the blackleaded grate and Martha prayed fervently for the things that Lottie had mentioned. When they got to their feet, and a cup of tea was on hand, Martha gave Lottie a warm invitation to come to the meeting next Sunday at The Salvation Army.

The following Sunday night, the evening service was well under way, when the door opened and Lottie, clad in her clogs and shawl appeared. It was to be the first of many such attendances, and the Army had gained an unusual and warmhearted follower. But she still enjoyed her drink with her mates down at The Rose and Crown and would gladly regale any company with a song at unexpected moments — such as the 'Testimony time' at the 'Army Praise Meeting' when she stood up and sang 'The Grandfather Clock'.

But one Sunday night a more solemn Lottie knelt at the altar in The Salvation Army hall and asked God to forgive her sins. Martha was there to help and encourage her, and she saw a change in Lottie's life that only Jesus Christ could bring about.

It was pretty obvious then that a change of job would have to be made and Lottie agreed that she would have to leave the pub if she was ever to take a hold on her drinking habits. She knew her weakness only too well. She soon found a new job washing dishes in a café and seemed happily settled there until matters got out of hand. Never having eaten an 'apple charlotte' in her life, Lottie thought the many orders for this popular pudding, shouted down the hatch from the café upstairs, was the staff making fun of her. One lunchtime it got too much for her and when the cook asked her if she liked apple charlotte she upped and punched him in the eye.

'Take that from apple charlotte,' she shouted — and was sacked on the spot for her unseemly behaviour.

Poor Lottie! When Martha explained to her what apple charlotte really was, she was amazed. She had acted out of total ignorance, for though she was impetuous she was not normally aggressive. She was one of the gems that Martha thanked God for and kept in touch with long after she left Ardwick.

Through all the wartime vicissitudes they had experienced together, the people of Ardwick had become very dear to Martha, the children especially, and she was sorry when the Marching Orders came for her to go to Everton

Slum Post, Liverpool. She took to Liverpool her new official rank of Adjutant – soon to be changed to Senior Captain. She took also her assistant officer, now Captain Bewick, who had been such a tremendous support in the work.

6

'A Proper Existence'

Tim O'Leary looked down at the threepenny bit in his grubby palm, then wiped his nose on his sleeve before turning his pale, dirt-streaked face up to Adjutant Field.

'Please, miss, I'd rather 'ave a slice of bread, ta.'

Martha looked at his thin frame and wished she'd thought of it herself. In thanks for Tim's help in running an errand to the Juvenal Street Market, she had automatically offered him a little pocket money. Yet she knew how hungry many of the children were who came to the Clifton Street Goodwill Centre in Everton, and how difficult it was for some families to keep body and soul together.

She called Tim inside, cut him a thick slice of bread with butter and jam, and watched him gobble it up, such was his hunger. His thin chest was barely covered by a shrunken grey sweater with holes at the elbows, and he wore grey trousers that were too long and threadbare at the knees. His socks and boots were equally inadequate against the chill cold.

For herself Martha didn't mind the physical hardships that six years of war had brought, but for the thin, neglected waifs, playing in the rubble and the gutters outside the Slum Post, she minded very much. They had never known anything better, because life in the slums of Liverpool as in most cities of the industrial North, was 'chill, damp, grey, gritty, smokey and brutal' as one commentator on the north-west put it.

Certainly the war had buffeted and scarred the already unattractive face of Liverpool with bomb craters, stretches of rubble and wasteland, derelict buildings and boarded-up houses.

To Martha and Winnie the damage in Everton appeared much worse than in Ardwick, and the people seemed somehow harder. It was ironic that they should have been sent to Everton at all. Whenever they had thought of the future beyond Ardwick, Martha's cry had been 'Anywhere but Liverpool, Lord . . .' The Slum Post at Everton, she knew to be a 'tough job', and it had been a considerably older and more experienced officer than the thirty-five-year-old Adjutant Field, who had been in charge there for eleven years, an unusually long time.

Clifton Street near the Juvenal Street market, and the city centre, was reputed to be in one of Liverpool's toughest areas. Nearby flowed the River Mersey with its bankside docks and Bootles' warehouses.

Martha and Winnie had known some hard times but those early days at Everton were, as Martha put it, 'a proper existence'. It was not just that the two women themselves had barely enough, but, more important, they were unable to obtain all they required to help the needy. Even basic necessities like bread, potatoes and coal, were in short supply. There was no money for the little extras that helped to soften a hard lot. Right from the start Martha was on the go seeing to the needs of the sick and the elderly. Trimming the paraffin lamps in the tall, overcrowded houses took her into some pitiful homes. The room of one old woman in her eighties, was typical. She lived alone in that one room without gas or electricity, and was dependent on the Salvation Army officers to keep an eye on her and light her lamp in the evenings. From bitter experience Martha learnt never to go into that poor woman's room until she had stamped loudly outside on the landing to frighten away the rats. But once inside, the occupant was always grateful to Martha for coming and thanked God for all His goodness to her.

It was not just light that the old people needed, of course. They needed warmth as well. Coal was difficult to obtain so Martha and the boys in the Sunday school would go round the market collecting empty crates and boxes. Then, while the lads chopped up the wood for kindling, Martha and Winnie made toffee apples for them with their precious ration of sugar. The firewood was distributed to the old people when they next called on them.

Washing and blanket-bathing the old people was often rewarding. Getting into the wrinkles on the old people's faces was usually a revelation!

Scrubbing out rooms was a chore that called for a great amount of energy. There was often only one tap for the whole house, and water had to be carried up and down narrow staircases, and there were no detergents such as we now have to make the task easier. Soda crystals or disinfectants, which made the hands sting, were best. But Martha discovered one vital 'commodity' in Everton — the Liverpool 'char'! No-one she met in all her years in goodwill work could scrub like Liverpool charladies, many of whom had been cleaners on the ocean liners at the port. They worked hard and did a thorough job. The big combustion stove in the hall at the Goodwill Centre provided not only heat but occasionally also a place to bake potatoes for the children. Hot lunches were served from the centre for the old people and on special occasions like Harvest and Christmas there would be festivities.

When Winnie Bewick's father was taken ill and she was

called home to Sunderland, Captain Euphemia Millar took her place at Everton. She arrived at the beginning of the severe flu epidemic of 1950–51.

Having worked extremely hard alongside her colleague caring for the sick, Captain Millar planned a well-earned break with her family at New Year in Scotland, and right up to the last moment she was 'on the job'.

'Eh Captain, will you come? Will you come?' An anxious woman rushed in through the back door just as Millar was picking up her bags to go to the railway station. 'It's me auntie, she's very poorly. I think she's dying.'

Captain Millar was about to put down her luggage when Martha, appearing in the doorway, intervened, 'Now off you go, Captain, or you'll miss your train. Make sure you enjoy yourself. I'll go with Mrs. Baldwin here . . .'

Millar, exhausted and grateful, hurried down the street, leaving Martha to set out on what was to be a frequent and sad duty in the weeks ahead. Mrs. Baldwin's aunt was only one of some fourteen people that Martha laid out during that time. While Captain Millar was at home in Scotland she was stricken with 'flu as well, and could not return to assist. So Martha was on her feet day and night with hardly any time to stop for meals.

Imagine the deep concern of the newly-appointed Goodwill Secretary, Lt.-Colonel Thomas Jewkes, when he arrived at the Everton Goodwill Centre one weekend to find Martha, already weary from ten nights of interrupted sleep, and still in constant demand.

'Now Adjutant, you must rest,' he said as the telephone rang again to ask for her help. 'Is there no other minister or person who can help . . .?'

'I'll have to rush, Colonel,' Martha said, hastily washing down cheese and biscuits with a cup of tea. 'Dr. Pollock says there's two people dead at Number 8 and it's Saturday and there's no-one else he can ask. How can I refuse?'

Visiting the sick, laying out the dead and conducting funerals, while trying to maintain the meetings at the Slum Post, it was not surprising that Martha was feeling exhausted. She was grateful to the other women who helped her in ways such as sitting up with a sick person, while Martha tried to get a night of uninterrupted sleep.

In her weary state it was also a relief to meet Christian people, praising God instead of complaining.

Alice was one of these. At over seventy she had been attending the Goodwill Centre for many years. She had seen much hardship in her life and had learnt to be ready to put her hand to anything to earn an honest penny. Her list of jobs included being a 'knocker-up', a runner of messages, a newspaper deliverer and seller. Even in that bitterest of winters, with treacherous roads and inadequate clothing, Alice still managed to muster the energy to carry on.

A habit of hers was to call in at the centre for a bowl of soup on her round. 'Ee, Captain,' she would say, as she thawed her frozen fingers around the hot soup bowl, 'The Lord is good to me. The Lord is good to me.'

Martha looked at her and wondered afresh at the old woman's gratitude. Her bent figure was covered in several layers of threadbare grey rags, a torn grey shawl covered her head and shoulders from which her wizened face peeped out and her feet were clad in broken, old boots. She appeared to have little to be thankful for, and it was not altogether surprising that she finally succumbed to the dreaded 'flu bug.

Digging into the much-used secondhand clothing store, Martha was able to find her a better shawl and a stronger pair of boots. Alice had further cause to praise the Lord and the next Sunday evening, 'flu or no 'flu, she was in her usual place at the meeting, thanking God from a full heart for all His goodness, and asking him to help her, despite her shortcomings, to be a worthy follower of her Master.

That grim winter was brightened by Mrs. Jenkins' eightieth birthday.

'We must listen to "Have a Go", this week, Bewick,' Martha said as she stamped the slush from her boots after visiting on a snowy afternoon. 'She's over the moon, bless her. Wilfred Pickles has put her on the short list for his programme which has really made her birthday. And you'll never guess what she's going to sing for him?'

'Now let me think . . .' Bewick replied with a smile. 'It wouldn't by any chance be "There is a lady sweet and kind", would it?'

'Sure and how did you guess?' Martha asked in mock surprise, for Mrs. Jenkins sang only one secular song and that was it! Her voice could always be heard, too, at The Salvation Army meetings, for she enjoyed singing her praises to God each Sunday.

But the birthday thrill had a sad sequel, for as Mrs. Jenkins was returning from the recording of the radio programme she was taken ill. Martha called in as soon as she heard the news, and found her lying on the sofa downstairs under some old blankets, her cat curled up by her feet. The room was chilly and poorly furnished, but spotlessly clean.

The old woman's face was pinched with exhaustion and pain and only with great effort could she talk. Martha busied herself making her more comfortable and checking to see that she had all she needed. 'Oh, Captain,' Mrs. Jenkins said, struggling to smile. 'Do you know I'm so fortunate. Why I've got all I want just here . . .' She tried to wave her arm but she was too weak. 'There's me 'ome, food to eat, me friends — and Timmy here. I'm just praising God for all that e's given me . . .'

She paused to take another shuddering breath and her lids drooped. Martha quietly put the kettle on the stove and settled herself down, for she expected to stay with the old lady that night. It was obvious Mrs. Jenkins had overtaxed her strength and was seriously ill. In fact Martha's vigil lasted on and off for the best part of a week, and she was challenged not only by the old lady's gratitude to God for the little she had, but also by her wonderful confidence that God was going to take her to Himself. Her simple faith was an inspiration.

Martha became used to caring for the sick but poverty — particularly when it affected little children — was still hard for her to witness. She was haunted by the conditions under which one family were living. They had called at the Goodwill Centre because they were troubled about their sick baby girl. Martha accompanied them home — if you could call it that. In one room lit only by a candle, there was no furniture except for two beds with no bedding. A make-shift table had been created by placing what looked like the remnants of a door across a wooden crate. On the 'table' was a full bottle of milk and half a slice of dry bread and that appeared to be all.

In the room were two infants. The elder girl, only eighteen months old, happily clutched a dirty but much-loved rag doll. The younger child, a six-weeks-old girl was crying bitterly, and when Martha picked her up her condition was quite worrying. She was hot and breathed heavily.

Arranging for the doctor to see the baby, Martha determined to do something about that room. She managed to secure sheets, blankets and a table from The Salvation Army red shield service (founded for the welfare of servicemen). Food was bought for the family also and toys for the two children. The doctor diagnosed a severe bout of enteritis and the baby was admitted to hospital immediately.

Poverty amongst the old people was more common and they could get themselves into a terrible state through neglect. One dark February evening found Martha, with the aid of a torch, climbing the dark, rickety stairs of a derelict house, just off Scotland Road. A call had come for her to care for a sick old man. But she little expected such squalid conditions. The house had no sanitation for a start, and as Grandad Kemp lived in a top back room, he had not bothered much about such things anyway. When Martha first entered his room a fearful stench engulfed her. After a moment or two, she overcame her first wave of revulsion and began to try and discover why the old man had let himself get in this state. He must see a doctor, she said, hoping in that way to make sure that Grandad was moved to hospital.

The doctor came to remonstrate with the old man but nothing they could say would persuade him to go to hospital. He was not going to be moved.

Martha's heart sank. If Grandad Kemp stayed, it was obviously going to be the Slum Officers' job to see he was cleaned up, and there was not a drop of water in the house.

Popping home to Clifton Street she called for Winnie's assistance — heating water in kettles and pans, then carrying it around the corner and down the street and up the narrow stairs. The soiled bed and bedclothes were burned outside in the backyard and before a secondhand bed was moved in, the scrubbing began. While Martha cleaned the floors, Winnie washed the old man. Then, with the room sparkling and his skin pink and white for the first time for a very long time, they thought that all he could possibly want was a hot meal and a cup of tea.

But there was just one more thing — his clay pipe. Grandad was grateful to the two Salvation Army lassies for 'doing him proud', but would they just light his pipe for him before they left?

Martha's experience of lighting pipes was not vast, but she knew that usually tobacco went in the bowl. She asked him where it was. 'Oh, no, chick,' he cackled. 'Ain't got no baccy. Got no money for it. Here, put a few tea leaves in.'

So Martha tried a few dry tea leaves without much success, partly because she didn't know Grandad should have been sucking at the pipe, when she was holding a lighted match to the bowl. Despite this failure, Grandad was grateful for their continued care in what proved to be his last days.

7

Liverpool's Likely Lads

For all its toughness, life in Liverpool was seldom dull. Many a Saturday night in the pubs and outside, there was trouble. And it was the Salvation Army lassies, not the police, who invariably got called in to calm things down. The street fighting of rival factions was the worst.

'Will you come and take hold of a man's feet?' a distraught woman asked when they answered her loud knocking late one Saturday night. Martha and Winnie had just got into the quarters from pub booming, and had been looking forward to a cup of tea.

'To be sure I will,' Martha agreed, putting on her bonnet again and following the woman down the street, wondering whether 'the feet' were alive or dead. She was no more certain when she arrived on the edge of a terrifying mêlée of men, shouting abuse and obscenities and hitting one man lying defenceless on the ground. Left to it, Martha felt sure they would soon kill him, and the police seemed unable to do anything.

Martha pushed her way into the crowd. Knocking arms and elbows aside as she went, she reached the man and grasped his ankles. The crowd, a little astonished at her appearance and quietened by the sight of her uniform, fell back, leaving the man alone. As Martha tended him the police came forward and managed to disperse the stragglers.

The Divisional Commander at the time, Colonel Ernest Fewster, visited the Everton Goodwill from time to time to conduct meetings for Martha, and both he and his wife were impressed by the crowd of Liverpudlians—of all persuasions—that were drawn to the centre by their affection for her. Colonel Fewster felt sure her Irish humour and wit had no little part to play in this.

On the whole denominationalism was something that didn't bother Martha and Winnie too much. The Salvation Army was able to offer help to whoever was in need. But Liverpool certainly introduced Martha to one new religious ceremony, 'churching'. She had never heard of this Church of England service for the 'Thanksgiving of Women after Childbirth' before. Nor did she know the tradition (or superstition?) which maintained that if the new mother's first excursion outside the maternity ward or the home was not to be 'churched' then dreadful bad luck would fall on her and the newborn child. Martha's Church of Ireland background, and her Salvation Army experience, had done little to prepare her for this particular request, made by one of the mothers from the Home League.

'I want to be churched, Captain,' she asked, when Martha visited her after the birth of her baby.

'Churched?' Martha looked startled. 'What's that then? I've not heard of it before.'

'Oh you know,' Mrs. Mason answered. 'I can't cut a piece of bread until I've been to the House of the Lord—and be prayed for, like?'

'Well,' Martha said. 'You can come to the House of the Lord this afternoon, and I'll gladly "church" you; but to tell you the truth, it's all new to me.'

Not to be put off, Mrs. Mason came to the Army Hall with her baby and Martha, taking courage, prayed for

God's blessing on her, thanking Him for the safe delivery of the child. Not knowing quite what was expected of her next, she prayed for the family and the upbringing of the little one.

Eventually she stopped and saw that Mrs. Mason's face was a trifle perplexed. 'Is everything all right, love? Have I done what you wanted me to do?' Martha asked her anxiously.

Mrs. Mason looked even more troubled. 'Oh, yes. It was luvely, ta. But it's me wots all wrong. I'm all uncomfortable inside and want to get it sorted out . . .'

So they sat side by side in the Hall and Martha gently probed for the real cause of her worry. 'I want to give myself but I know I'm not good enough, see? And I don't know how.'

As they talked on Martha realised her genuine longing to come to God. She explained to her simply what God had done in Jesus Christ and what she must do in response to God's love. Mrs. Mason, obviously prompted by the Holy Spirit, responded. Having become a Christian she was a tremendous support to the work they were doing at Everton. What was more, she soon had her friends and neighbours queueing to be 'churched' in the afternoons as soon as they were discharged from the Mothers' Hospital in the morning. Martha was amazed, as she told Winnie afterwards, 'Well, Bewick. I've never known anything like this before. The Lord really used that little service and there was I — not sure what to do for the best!'

There is little doubt that one of the highlights of the weekly routine for Martha and Winnie at Everton was the Sunday school — a big one numbering some eighty boys and girls and divided into two sessions. The 'scouse kids' provided many exasperating yet hilarious moments. Some were from Irish families, and quite a large proportion came from difficult or poverty-stricken homes. Many parents could not afford to take their children away on holiday, or even a day's outing, and Everton's bomb-scarred landscape did not provide much scope for play and recreation. So special efforts were made by the two officers to get the children away from the smog and grime of Liverpool and into the comparatively fresh air of the surrounding districts.

The Liverpool lads certainly had their own native wit and charm, which would catch Martha and Winnie unawares and have them biting their lips to stop laughing out loud in moments of solemnity. The incident that was to live in their memories the longest and never failed to reduce them to tears of laughter when retold, was over the ten secondhand fur coats. These were discovered in a Salvation Army depot, and handed to the Goodwill Officers for distribution. The coats weren't particularly beautiful, but they were warm, and in the bitter cold they would be more than useful.

One by one Martha found ten old ladies among those in touch with the Centre, who needed warm overcoats. However, one fitting proved difficult. Mrs. Randall, whom they visited regularly at home, had always appeared thin and frail. When she came to Clifton Street to try on her coat, the small-sized garment they had selected for her would not meet round her middle. Closer inspection revealed why. Round her waist was tied a canvas bag containing the contents of her larder. The explanation was a simple and obvious one, as far as Mrs. Randall was concerned. 'It's my old man, Captain. Eighty-four last birthday and him with an appetite like an 'orse. Never knows when he's had enough. As soon as my back is turned he eats anything he can lay 'is 'ands on, see.'

The old ladies, tall or short, fat or thin, were thrilled with their 'furs', even if their old felt hats and boots did not match, or the coats hung loosely on their short figures, what did it matter? They felt like royalty. And when Sunday came, a procession of be-furred elderly ladies began to arrive at the Hall for the meeting. As each one entered and sat down Martha and Winnie had increasing difficulty in keeping back the smiles, for it was not just that they looked less than smart but also that they hadn't realised that so many others were as fortunate as themselves. As each one arrived, they got the 'I know where you got that from' look and, sitting down, would look round and see others dressed in the same way as themselves.

It had been hard suppressing their mirth before the meeting, but worse was to follow. Martha thought she had her feelings well under control when she came to start the service. But as she called to Tommy to close the door so that they could begin proceedings, any attempt to remain dignified, was ruined by his cheerful, 'I can't Captain, there's another gorilla coming!'

Amidst all the post-war pressures on the work at Everton, Martha found, as the 1940's passed and in came the 1950's, that her heart was turned more and more to home. Her mother's health was worrying her, for a decline was evident on each trip to Belfast. The time was drawing near, Martha felt sure, when her mother would need special nursing at home. With her married sister still in Canada, it was naturally upon Martha that her mother depended. Fortunately Martha's concern was not unknown to Colonel Muirhead, the Head of the Goodwill Work, and when the Belfast Goodwill Post needed a new Commanding Officer, it was Senior Captain Martha Field who was appointed there in May 1951, Festival of Britain year.

It was a vastly different Belfast to which the forty-year-old Martha returned to live, after an absence of seventeen years. Modern motorbuses ran over the old tram routes, and after the destruction of the war, some fine new roads and civic buildings had been built.

But the post-war years were proving not entirely happy ones for the hitherto prosperous industrial city. Though the war had given a tremendous boost to the engineering and shipbuilding enterprises, the post-war boom was beginning to fade. And the third largest industry, linen-spinning, was hit the hardest. By 1951 the huge backlog in world demand for textiles had been met and the order books were emptying. In July 1952 over 10,000 linen workers were unemployed, and this was the beginning of a gradual decline in all the industries. Added to this rising unemployment problem, Belfast had managed to become desperately overcrowded, with a subsequent shortage of housing and public facilities. The 1951 census revealed that 440,000 people were squeezed into the small inner city area, and many of the homes that Martha was to visit were affected by these factors, with poverty and deprivation worsened by unemployment.

8

Belfast Once More

During Martha's years at Everton The Salvation Army, recovering from the demands of the war, had taken stock of itself sufficiently to pay tribute to a notable anniversary in 1947: the Diamond Jubilee of the Slum and Goodwill Work. The occasion was marked by special celebrations, held in mid-October, including a rally in the Regent Hall, Oxford Street, London, and an exhibition at the recently-opened Hoxton Goodwill Centre, where some of Hugh Redwood's dreams of a Goodwill League in action were coming true.

His vision was of a League open to volunteers, of all denominations, who would work with the Army to bring 'to those in greatest need the pooled resources of a membership ready to make its utmost contributions, whether in time or money, in manual labour or professional skill, in teaching or tending, in needlework or nursing, edification or amusement — according to the qualifications of each.' All this came to be summed up in the Goodwill League's motto 'Such as I have give I'.

The first new 'Goodwill Centre' at Hoxton Martha would hardly recognise. It was a large purpose-built community centre providing opportunities for work, food and shelter, recreation and instruction, healing and mending, cleansing and comforting, all under one roof, which itself was a playground. The building contained a kitchen, laundry, sewing room, day nursery, club rooms for adults of various ages, flats for the homeless and a chain of clinics. Not least, of course, was a beautifully appointed hall for meetings. The full-time staff at the centre was a small one, for part-time Goodwill League volunteers gave their time and talents gladly.

In the special illustrated programme for the celebrations the past, present and future of the work were mentioned, paying special tribute to the two Slum Officers who had died with their people during the London blitz, Captain Jessie North and Lieutenant Edith Stead. The question was asked, 'But surely the slums can't be as bad now as they were sixty years ago?' The Army's reply was courteous but firm. 'What about the revelations which slum evacuees pressed upon our reluctant eyes during wartime evacuation of our cities a few years ago? People are not changed by Acts of Parliament. Higher wages do not always bring about a better domestic life and scene. The 1947 Slum Officer still finds in plenty, neglected children, squalid homes, the helpless aged, the sick, the worried, the wretched, awaiting her ministrations. And in these ministrations she is still the evangelist first of all . . .'

Hugh Redwood, of course, had a special place of honour in the Jubilee programme and paid his own tribute: 'Very nearly twenty years have passed since I made the acquaintance of the officers of the Slum Department on the occasion of a Thames-side disaster. Looking back, indeed it seems as if the whole current of my life changed there, in the back streets of Westminster, though in fact the change had occurred in the previous year, and this was rather the coming of opportunity.

'Opportunity! To what countless numbers of people has it been brought by the service and example of these splendid workers for Christ. Even in twenty years I have seen it come to all sorts and conditions in all manner of ways, and twenty years is only one-third of the period for which the work has been done.

'There is a vast field still before the department. Changing conditions call for changing methods and probably for new departmental names. But the name which is above all other names stands unchanged and unchangeable as the only one in which the hope of fullness of life can be realized. Fundamental needs are the same, and post-war conditions have tended to aggravate them rather than otherwise. But we preach Jesus, the power of God and the wisdom of God to deal with them at their worst.'

When Martha's move to Belfast was made, the parting with Everton friends and Winnie Bewick in particular, was sad. But to be in Grosvenor Road Slum Post, with her own home only a short bus-ride away was a wonderful relief. It meant, though, that while coping with many other demands for home nursing, sick visiting around the Falls Road, and running the meetings at the Post, Martha had to be ready to give help at home if her mother needed her. She slept at the quarters, but spent her spare moments at home.

Martha's mother was overjoyed to have her daughter back again after the years of separation, though unhappily they were to be together for only eleven months. Mrs. Field's battle for life finally ended in May 1952, despite the devoted loving nursing Martha gave her. It seemed to Martha that she had barely finished attending to the funeral and family matters, when disaster struck the city in the shape of severe floods.

Belfast's overcrowded low-lying residential and dockland areas were inundated with floodwater in the summer of 1952 and many made homeless. Martha, always at her best in emergencies, rushed with her Lieutenant to assist in the relief work, visiting upwards of a thousand homes in the area in the space of three weeks, supplying clothes, bed-linen, blankets, hot drinks and food, and even false teeth! The most desperate need was for clothing, to replace that swept away or ruined by floodwater. One poor mother-to-be saw a complete layette disappear as a cupboard was washed away. Martha was especially glad to be able to supply her with a new set.

Many of the homes they visited were also badly affected by mud and slime as the waters receded. Furniture, carpets, kitchen equipment, as well as walls and floors, needed cleaning and drying out or repairing. Most of all the distressed people wanted comfort, and Martha with her humour and cheerful practicality was a tower of strength. Even though she was emotionally and physically exhausted herself, she managed to keep going.

Of course, she was not alone. Besides Lieutenant Morgan there were Martha's colleagues from the Ballymacarrett Goodwill Post, and the officers and helpers from Divisional Headquarters and other corps. In fact, God provided for the crisis in a wonderful way. Barely a few hours before the floods struck, Major John Fewster, Divisional Commander in Belfast, had received an urgent telephone call from a baker in the city. Due to the death of a relative he was having to close his shop at short notice. Could The Salvation Army use 200 or more loaves of bread?

Major Fewster rang the officer in charge of the men's hostel who readily accepted them, uncertain of quite how he was going to use them all. When the floods came the bread was immediately available for distribution to the hundreds of people whose homes and larders had been destroyed.

Checking up on one house affected by the floodwaters, Martha and her Lieutenant discovered an elderly man in a very weakened state. Martha recognised the signs of an advanced case of tuberculosis — the cough, the wasted frame, the deep-socketed eyes, and at first thought it was fever that seemed to excite him, when they entered his damp uncared-for bedroom. As she ministered to his needs he explained brokenly that he had been a Salvationist but had drifted away, and they were the first Salvation Army officers to visit his home for seventeen years. The tears came to his eyes as he thanked them for coming, and both girls found it hard to fight back their own tears as they listened to his tale of loneliness and failure. Mr. Murphy was visited regularly after that, and was able to thank God for bringing the two officers into his life, through the floods.

It was amazing how the local community was united by the disaster and forgot their petty differences. The Grosvenor Road Goodwill Centre ('Slum Post' had been officially dropped as a name by this time) was just off Falls Road, a largely Roman Catholic area of the city. The Goodwill Officers maintained an open attitude, befriending and helping people of all persuasions. But in the floods, Catholics and Protestants pulled together, to help those in need; and the Goodwill Officers gave assistance to both.

While waiting at a bus stop one Saturday, Martha saw a man on the other side of the road stumble, then fall to the ground. It was almost lunchtime and the street was empty of passers-by. Martha crossed the road to help the barely conscious man lying still unnoticed on the pavement. As soon as she reached him she recognised the Roman Catholic priest who was a teacher at the nearby boys' school.

He was obviously very ill and Martha did what little she could for him, while someone ran for the police and called an ambulance. Someone else ran for the Cardinal but meanwhile Martha put her coat beneath his head and her arm around his shoulders. His eyelids fluttered in distress and she noticed his hand weakly fumbling in his robes.

Putting her hand into his pocket she found his crucifix and gently closed his feeble fingers around it, holding it close to his eyes as he died. The Cardinal sadly arrived after the ambulance. At the sight of a Salvation Army officer tending a priest, Martha overheard one policeman remark, 'I never thought to see such a thing!'

Quite early one chilly autumn morning Martha was disturbed by a knocking and sobbing outside the front door of the quarters. The small boy on the doorstep was crying so hard she assumed he had fallen down and hurt his knee. While she waited for his sobs to subside she made him a glass of orange juice.

'There now, pet, what's wrong? Have you hurt yourself?'

'I'se come lookin' for you last night,' he hiccuped and swallowed back a sob. 'And you'se wasn't here.' He wept again, rubbing the tears away with his shirt sleeve. 'Mum's gone off and left us, and now Dad's very sick . . . and I tried to cook the breakfast . . . and the eggs wouldn't work. . .' The tears took over afresh.

Michael was right. Martha and Lieutenant Morgan had been out the night before at the midweek Divisional Holiness meeting. Hastily gathering some food together, and packing her bag, Martha went to Michael's home to see what could be done.

She found Mr. Casey upstairs very sick indeed, and called the doctor. Then she investigated the back room downstairs — three children were peering round the scullery door as she came down. There was an ominous smell of burnt cooking and when she entered the kitchen she could count twelve eggshells. Michael's efforts at breaking eggs had been no more successful than his efforts at frying them!

The doctor arrived and decided that Mr. Casey should be moved to Isolation Hospital. The four children looked even more lost and Martha could not bear to see them parcelled out to an institution. With the Children's Officer's permission she and Lieutenant Morgan took them home to Grosvenor Road as a temporary measure while their father's health improved and their future was decided. With Christmas coming Martha took every opportunity to 'mother' them, and see what could be done to brighten their lives. They were invited to spend Christmas Day at the Goodwill Centre, all four children receiving a present from the brightly decorated tree.

In the comparatively brief three-year appointment at the Belfast Goodwill Centre, from May 1951 to May 1954 Martha was able to renew acquaintance with good friends who were appointed in charge of The Salvation Army corps at Bangor, soon after Martha took up the reins of her work at Belfast. The new officers had barely settled into their bungalow when the telephone rang. It was Martha to ask how they were settling in, though her call was prompted by a strong desire to talk to someone about a terrible problem.

'I'm desperate. Do you think you can help me? I've got a little girl here and she does need a holiday. I must get her away. She needs a lot of love and reassurance. Would you be knowing anyone who could take her?'

'Why of course, Field,' her friend said, thinking hard because they were only just getting to know the local people, and off-hand she could not name anyone. 'What's the trouble?'

Martha poured out one of the saddest stories that either woman had ever heard. She visited by request, the girl's mother in hospital, where she had just given birth to her eighth child and found the woman in great distress and desperate for help. Betty, aged thirteen, who was her eldest daughter, had been found at school to be pregnant, her own father being responsible for her condition. The girl had had to go through the ordeal of giving evidence in court against him, seen him found guilty and given nine years' imprisonment. Her confinement had been very difficult, and the baby had survived only a few weeks. It was essential now, when she was to be discharged from hospital, that she should have a chance to get right away from the home and her past.

When Martha had finished, her friend said, 'Look love. I'll have a chat with my husband and make a few inquiries. But don't you worry yourself. If no-one else will have her, we will. Even if I have to share her with someone else.'

With two children of their own, the officers knew they had little space in the small bungalow, but after she and her husband had discussed the situation — and shed a few tears over the sad state of the young girl — they decided with a bit of a squeeze Betty could definitely come to them. Their children were told that Betty had been ill and very unhappy and were asked to help Mummy and Daddy to make her stay a happy one.

The day Betty went to Bangor was engraved on Martha's heart. The young girl, pale, silent, unexcited, sat quiescent in the car, not taking any notice of anything. Then, as they drove past the Law Courts she suddenly broke down, burying her face in her hands and saying, 'Oh don't ever let me see that horrible place again.' Martha hugged her close until the building which had such unhappy memories, was out of sight.

When they arrived at the bungalow in Bangor, the family's warm welcome produced little response. The unsmiling girl seemed old before her time and did not react as a thirteen-year-old should.

The bungalow was only five minutes from the seashore, and every effort was made to entertain their guest by walking, swimming and paddling expeditions, or picnic and sand castle outings. The young daughter of the house went out of her way to make Betty smile: her chief method — to let Betty sit beside her on the piano stool while she did her piano practice. She was talented musically, and glad to have a 'pupil' whom she could encourage. Betty slowly began to respond. The fresh air, the new surroundings, the music and the friendliness of the family helped her to relax and try to forget the past. The whole family rejoiced the day they actually saw Betty smile.

9

Notice to Quit

Disbelievingly Martha read the words on the piece of paper again: 'You are hereby given notice to quit these premises by Monday, 2nd August, 1954, at the latest . . .'

That was impossible. It was only two days hence. She and her assistant, Captain Day, had been in Greenock only a few weeks and here was a dreadful threat to their work — and with barely two days' notice? Martha had come to the hall to prepare for the Sunday meetings, only to find they had to be out on the Monday, which happened to be a Bank Holiday. She had better act now or not at all.

'Oh Lord, help me please to find a way round this,' she prayed as she set out. As a stranger to Greenock and not yet knowing many people Senior Captain Field took herself for advice to the local police station. How her heart lifted to hear the cheerful Irish brogue of the constable on duty!

His suggestion that she take her case to the Provost seemed a good one but Martha trembled at the thought of bothering such an illustrious person, until the policeman offered to make the introduction for her. Lo and behold! Provost Boyd was also Irish! She not only gained a sympathetic hearing but he also looked into the situation immediately.

Apparently the people from whom The Salvation Army rented the hall in Cathcart Street had sold it to a local firm as a television store. But with Provost Boyd's good offices a delay of a precious month was obtained before the new tenants would want the premises.

A month seemed quite a long time when Martha set out with high hopes on her search for a new hall or base for the goodwill work. She and Captain scoured the 'To Let' columns of the *Greenock Telegraph* every day. Every spare moment they were telephoning, examining property and checking addresses. The local Corps assisted them in their search as well, and when Captain Day was appointed elsewhere, Martha particularly appreciated their support.

But the end of August approached and all her efforts to find somewhere proved fruitless. 'All we need,' she assured one man she stopped in the street in her desperation, 'is a room large enough to hold meetings, and help people. Surely someone in Greenock can provide us with that? Would you know of anywhere?' The man shook his head sadly — not able to think of any solution to her dilemma . . .

Poor Martha. Out from early morning until late afternoon, with the rain tippling down from leaden skies, the smallest thing seemed a crowning blow. When she arrived back at the quarters cold, tired, lonely and very discouraged, the sight of her sodden stockings and the hole in her only decent pair of shoes was just too much. She sat and wept bitterly.

She tried to dry out and patch the shoes and keep a hold on herself, telling the Lord that she knew He must have a purpose in all this — but what? Next day she was out again, trudging the streets making futile telephone calls or journeys. She returned tired and dejected once again to the tenement flat in Lynedoch Street.

A ring at the doorbell and a call from below startled her,

for it was dark and late for callers. Going down the narrow stairs the sight of the gentleman she had waylaid in the street was an even greater surprise. He and his wife had come specially to tell her of a possible suite of rooms to be rented in Kilblain Street. They belonged to the Good Templars (a temperance society) of which he was a member. Would they be of any use to the Army?

Martha was overwhelmed by their kind thought in taking the trouble to find her, and expressed her gratitude and immediate interest while pressing them to come in for a cup of tea. Sitting in the cramped 'quarters' Mr. Blair went on to describe the rooms and mentioned a very reasonable rent which included the use of the electric light. He admitted that the place had not been in use for some time, but should The Salvation Army want it, they would see to the redecoration.

Martha longed to say 'yes' right away. The month's reprieve was up and already her precious organ and song-books had been put out on the pavement once in the rain. Fortunately friends who attended the Goodwill Centre had seen what had happened and had been able to cover them up and move them indoors again. What was more important, the goodwill work had to go on somewhere. Even if this suite of rooms did need decorating, she could hold cottage meetings in people's homes in the meantime.

Remembering that Headquarters would be paying the rent and would need the reassurance that Senior Captain Field had inspected the premises *before* she said 'yes', she arranged to view them the next day — and was relieved to find them suitable, though musty from disuse. Gladly she could agree the final details and begin to arrange the move from Cathcart Street.

In some ways it was a sad end to the work there, for it was the breaking of a historic link with the past, as Martha well knew. The hall had been what The Salvation Army termed a 'glory shop', where amazing conversions had taken place among the tough dockers and shipbuilding workers of the Greenock area, many of them heavy drinkers. The Cathcart hall, now destined to house television sets, had rung to 'Hallelujah' and 'Praise the Lord' and rousing triumphant singing.

But if the 'glory shop' was no more, it was certainly not to be the end of the Army's influence in Greenock. In many ways the next few years were crucial as the new Goodwill Centre was established in Kilblain Street, and Martha faced a major test as she started her work in the new premises that lacked much of the 'character' of the old hall.

She felt very differently however as, weary yet exhilarated, she climbed the uneven stairs to the dingy, badly-lit top floor rooms of her quarters. Never before had she had to work in one place and live in another. All her previous appointments had involved 'living over the shop', or to be more accurate, over the converted pub. Now she had to walk from East to West Greenock to get to the Goodwill Centre. Furthermore the cramped conditions, poor sanitation and damp, draughty rooms at Lynedoch Street, did not help matters. Yet, she reminded herself, many of their people had to live in very similar — or worse — conditions, so why should not she?

With the need to establish the new Goodwill Centre occupying all her energies, Martha did not see herself moving quarters in a hurry. Gradually the weekday routine built up and the Sunday meetings resumed their normal pattern. When her new assistant, Lieutenant Lindsay, joined her in November visiting got under way in earnest. A large number of elderly and sick people came to recognise and love the cheery Irish voice of Senior Captain Field or the warm Glaswegian lilt of her Lieutenant.

Thursday lunchtimes were soon occupied with cooking

and serving hot lunches to the old people, while the youngsters were not forgotten. A weekly boys' club provided games and refreshments, building on the experiences of Manchester and Liverpool. The Home League met on Tuesday afternoons and Martha and Dorothy grew to appreciate the Scottish women's warm hospitality. Any requests for help with secondhand goods or clothing were generously met, and their home-made oatcakes, shortbreads and scones were mouthwateringly good.

This was Martha's first taste of life in Scotland. Greenock, though much smaller than Belfast, was largely dockland and slum. Shipyards, including the famous 'Tail of the Bank', warehouses and factories sprawled along the four-mile waterfront, with the narrow streets of tall tenements climbing up the slope behind, away from the Firth of Clyde to where Loch Thom and the Gryfe Reservoir provided water for the area. Glasgow was twenty-three miles away to the east beyond Port Glasgow, while going west an esplanade extended from Princes Pier, Greenock, to Fort Matilda on the boundary of Gourock at the mouth of the Firth. The war and the blitz had left their mark on parts of the town — and the Cross of Lorraine memorial on Lyle Road paid tribute to the French seamen based at Glasgow who had lost their lives in the Battle of the Atlantic.

But there were gains in being stationed in a smaller place like Greenock (with only 78,000 inhabitants as compared with Belfast's 440,000) and in the centre of a town and not in one part of a larger city, as at Manchester and Liverpool. In Greenock, the 'Slum Sisters' as the local paper still always called them, were very much part of a tight-knit community.

A journalist on the local evening paper, the *Greenock Telegraph* gave them generous support, for one thing, and there were often weekly reports on the work of the Goodwill Centre. The Rev. James Dow was not only a journalist, however, he was also a local Church of Scotland minister who was clearly sympathetic with what The Salvation Army was doing in the community, and he wrote this regular feature.

Certainly one of his most trenchant 'exposés' at that time resulted from his knowledge of their crying need for better living quarters. As autumn 1955 took its course, Martha (promoted Major in May) and Captain Dorothy Lindsay found the Lynedoch Street rooms an increasing burden. It was a well-known local saying that 'the higher you went the cheaper the rent'; but it was just not worth saving the money when you were exhausted after a hectic day and had a fair distance to travel home. Why not apply to the local council for a flat, or house, someone suggested? With sufficient encouragement they did so, with high hopes of a positive response. They were turned down.

When James Dow came to hear of it he made it quite clear that he thought it a sad day for Greenock: 'Most people work a bit better when they get some encouragement,' he wrote in the *Greenock Telegraph.* 'Folk who give their lives to good works do not labour for the sake of the reward, and certainly not for any applause which their efforts may merit.

'But even the most humble, selfless and devoted doer of good likes to feel that the work does not pass unappreciated. For this reason, if for no other, the Corporation were wrong to turn down the Slum Sisters' application for a Corporation house without more inquiry . . . the application was turned down by the votes of people whose only knowledge of the Slum Sisters' work comes from hearsay.

'These specially trained and completely devoted women are in short supply in the ranks of The Salvation Army. It seems quite possible that the Army will deploy its limited forces in areas where the need is as great as Greenock's need, but where the work is appreciated a little more practically.'

Not content with that protest in print, the minister acted as well. Within a few weeks a number of events took place. An empty, nearly derelict detached house had been found in Regent Street, Greenock, and offered to The Salvation Army for a very small sum. Headquarters agreed to buy it, and into it moved a veritable army of volunteers to renovate it — all in response to an appeal for help published by James Dow and supported by at least one of the local councillors.

Local firms gave materials for fittings and furnishings: Scotts Shipbuilding provided most of the bathroom and sanitary equipment; Taylors & Taylors gave wallpaper and paint and a further kind donor presented a cooker for the kitchen. In all, sixteen tradesmen from very different backgrounds responded to the appeal. There were Roman Catholics, Salvationists, Church of Scotland members and non-churchgoers among them, but they worked together marvellously.

It was Martha's and Dorothy's habit to drop in on the men working in the empty house, usually with tea and scones to encourage them. One very cold night Martha saw a sight she was not to forget easily. As they came in the front door, the first thing that caught her eye was a minister's 'dog collar' looped round the handle of the kitchen door. Opening the door gingerly she and Dorothy peered round the edge. There was the Rev. James Dow in overalls, his face black with soot, helping an equally sooty-faced Alex McDonald (chief foreman joiner of Scotts shipbuilding), Duncan McCle (a master plasterer who had almost rebuilt the interior of the house) and Neil Thompson (another joiner) as they struggled to remove the old blacklead kitchen range to make way for the new cooker. Work soon stopped at the welcome sight of the women with a cup of tea, and much mopping of sooty brows with handkerchiefs took place.

After the construction work was finished, into the house moved the local ladies to scrub out the rooms. These hearty, 'sonsie' women reminded Martha of the Liverpool charladies who had warmed her heart with their hard work. The Scottish women seemed similarly happy to tackle any job however dirty, always joking, their humour infectious. Finally the furniture was installed in the new house, and the curtains hung with the help of one of the men.

The sense of satisfaction in a job well done pervaded the 'Grand Opening' on March 21st, 1956, with Lt.-Commissioner Robert Harewood from Glasgow Territorial Headquarters conducting the simple ceremony of thanksgiving and dedication. The key was officially 'turned' by the Rev. James Dow, and a tea provided for all the helpers and kind donors of materials. In all, sixty-four people sat down to eat, and Martha who had never held with 'high tables' where 'top brass' sat in state, was not going to start now. So the Commissioner sat next to the joiner, the Chief Secretary next to the plasterer and the ladies who had done the scrubbing sat next to the minister. In the photographs taken at the opening, a cheerful group of workers and helpers surround a smiling Martha and Dorothy, and the pictures of the renovated house show its new fittings gleaming with polish and care, vases of flowers decorating every room.

A picture was duly printed in the local paper with Martha's thanks to all concerned. Later the same paper reported 'For the past month now the Slum Sisters in Greenock have been operating in their 'new' house in Regent Street, which, in the words of one of the sisters 'is simply heavenly'. The two Salvation Army women have a room each, there is a large sitting-room, a bathroom and a kitchen, and most important of all to the sisters, a small, but comfortable, emergency room.

'Since they moved into the house this room has been occupied twice — once by a young Dundee woman and then by a young Glasgow girl. Both of them had had trouble at home. They were both cared for by the sisters and then sent to Glasgow to The Salvation Army Women's Hostel.

'Almost every day the sisters receive clothing for needy men, women and children from local residents. Although they do help young families who are having a bad time, most of the sisters' work is done among the old and infirm. They pay regular visits to many old people in Greenock and Port Glasgow, taking soup and other foodstuffs.'

A report of the opening also appeared in *The Deliverer*, The Salvation Army paper for women. Its editor, Brigadier Gladys Taylor, who had met Major Field for the first time in the new Greenock quarters, was impressed by the view of the Clyde from the front windows, and stood watching the big liners passing up and down. Martha, seeing her, told her of an incident that took place at the opening. One of the local Councillors, had looked up to see a big liner sailing majestically on its way out of the Clyde to the Irish Sea. He turned to Martha and said: 'You could ask us for that and I think the Council would give it to you.' Thanks to James Dow the Slum Officers had certainly made their mark locally.

As the *Greenock Telegraph* had reported, their greatest asset at Regent Street was the spare room. Though this was a new departure for Martha and Dorothy, it proved its worth right from the start. Besides the two girls referred to already the officers had also provided temporary accommodation for Jean, a sixteen-year-old runaway, whom the police asked them to care for. When she arrived Jean was hungry and physically a wreck, her hair matted, her clothes filthy and her face bruised. It transpired that she had been beaten up, though this might well have been partly her own fault, for as Martha sadly discovered, she was young in years, but old in crime.

Another evening saw a coloured girl and her baby coming for help and a bed for the night. Her husband had 'bad turns' and had threatened to kill her and the child. Not content with taking in the needy pair, Martha tackled her husband and persuaded him to have treatment.

The police knew the Salvation Army officers well and were often in touch or referred cases of need to them. One Friday evening, very late, with a gale blowing straight off the Clyde and the rain squalling against their front windows the two women heard a ring at the bell. Behind the police constable's tall figure five pairs of eyes peered pathetically out of drawn faces. Two small children lay huddled together in a pram which was crammed with cartons, foodstuffs and toys. Their mother held the pram, and clutching her arm were two older children nearly asleep on their feet.

She was horrified to discover that the family had been walking the streets for some hours. All were soaking wet and cold. The foodstuffs in the pram were ruined. While beds were made and baths arranged, hot drinks helped to thaw out the party and the mother explained her desperate situation. She had been that day to the Chest clinic for an X-ray report which had been discouraging. She must come in for treatment, she was told. How could she, with four children and a working husband, and no parents or relatives to help her? To crown everything, her husband, who was a heavy drinker, had come home that evening, having spent most of his wages in the pub, and in a matter of seconds had wrecked the poorly-furnished place she had struggled to keep clean and maintain as a home.

Not knowing where to go but unable to stand things any

longer, she had gathered up some belongings and stuffed them into the pram and left home. As she and the children trudged along the river embankment the gale began to blow her hair in her eyes and she took shelter in a telephone kiosk. Through her tears as she tied on a headscarf, she caught sight of some words in the telephone directory lying open in front of her. 'Where there's need there's The Salvation Army!' That's it, she thought. She had a need — she'd go to them.

She didn't know where the Goodwill Centre was, and just walked and walked, hoping to find it. Fortunately for all concerned they were stopped by a policeman, who not surprisingly wanted to know what they were doing out on such a night. It was he who brought them to the Centre.

The family stayed with the two officers until it was clear that the mother could have treatment without further anxiety, and a reconciliation had been brought about with her husband.

On another bitterly cold blustery night Martha and Dorothy were just locking up the hall in Kilblain Street, when a boy aged about eight arrived, looking strained and bewildered. He handed Martha a note from his father.

> 'As my wife has deserted me and I cannot cope with the children, I want The Salvation Army to look after my four bairns.'

Martha showed the letter to Dorothy, her face grave. She asked the boy his name.

'Jamie,' he said.

'Well, Jamie,' Martha said, putting her arm around his shoulders, 'Will you take me to your father, please? He wants to see me.'

Though it was well past his bedtime, Jamie kept up a

good pace as they walked through the dark streets. When they reached the house they found the other three children and their father very upset. He seemed to have gone to pieces. He claimed he had nothing more to live for now his wife had gone. What point was there in going on? He did not want the children to suffer and he could not cope with them himself. If the Salvation Army didn't take them he would not be responsible for the consequences. He would put all their heads in the gas oven—his own included!

Try as they could, the two officers could not calm him or reassure him. The children were distressed and if left would be at risk. Gathering up their nightclothes, Martha shepherded the disconsolate group to the quarters.

Having so little room for four children, Martha contacted the local Children's Officer, who was a Christian and especially glad to assist the two Salvation Army officers in their work. But in this instance, there seemed little she could do. They tried once again to reason with the father, but he was not even capable of holding down his job let alone coping with the children. One thing, however, that he was clear about: he wanted the children to remain in the care of the Army. Then Martha had a brainwave. Not far away in Gourock was a Salvation Army holiday home for tired mothers — she would ring there. Yes, they could take the children at least for a while.

Jamie and his brothers and sister were given a loving welcome at the Home by Major Wheatley and her new assistant, Captain Sophie Wilson—and it was the beginning of a new friendship for Martha as well as the children. Captain Wilson was soon to be appointed to assist Martha in her work—though neither of them knew it at that time.

It was sufficient that the plump auburn-haired officer took the four motherless children into her special care, and restored a bloom to their pale cheeks, as well as an occasional smile or two to their drawn faces. Regular bulletins were passed back to Martha at Greenock for the children's father, who had managed to resume work and would frequently drop in at the quarters for news of his children on the way.

One morning he did not call at the house, and Martha hastily made some inquiries. He had not appeared at work either and a neighbour had called the police to investigate. On breaking into the house the police found that he had hanged himself. It was a tragic situation and amidst their sadness, Martha was relieved that they had taken the children to safety.

For all the strides the Welfare State, the National Health Service and the Social Services were making in the mid-fifties, terrible poverty and sadness still came to light in Greenock, where overcrowding and slum conditions in old, badly-maintained tenements did not help matters. It was a new experience for Martha to work so closely with local social workers. The Welfare Officer in particular seemed glad to have the backing of the Goodwill Officers in his work. When needs went beyond the usual 'social' provisions he openly declared, 'I can do so much, but you have Jesus Christ. It makes all the difference.'

One family the Welfare Officer introduced to Martha consisted of ten people: parents and eight children — all living in one room — a kitchen! Not surprisingly the more time the children could spend away from those grim cramped conditions the more they liked it. But that led to mischief on the streets. Linda, the little girl of ten, was quick to learn a trick or two from her older sister, Jennifer, who at twelve had already been on probation for shoplifting and Linda was discovered one day by a policeman, begging for pennies outside the local pub. She was given a warning and put under the care of the Probation Officer, who longed to see the children get away from their home environment. Could The Salvation Army help?

Martha could give no immediate answer — but prayed about it. Unknown to her, friends of the Children's Officer who shared her concern, particularly for the two young girls, were about to become the answer to her prayer.

'Dear Major Field, we believe God wants us to open our home to a needy child from Greenock so that they can have a holiday. We have only just celebrated our first wedding anniversary, and have no children of our own yet. We thought we would like to do something practical to show how much God's love means to us. Do you think there is a child who would appreciate coming to stay with us?'

The Norrises, it transpired, had come to a living faith in Jesus Christ through hearing Billy Graham, the American evangelist, at Kelvin Hall in Glasgow, during his 1955 Crusade. They were unaware that their letter was quite so timely — and may have smiled at the alacrity with which Martha accepted their offer — wondering if they might just possibly be able to take two children instead of one.

10

Helping Greenock's Old and Young

It was not often that Martha's work met with opposition. Usually she had good reason to thank God for the support of local Christians and church people in Greenock. Besides the Good Templars and the trojan efforts of James Dow and his friends, there was the local doctor who gave two afternoons of her week, to help the Goodwill Officers in whatever way seemed best. As they had no transport and she had a car, it was a wonderful opportunity to visit cases further afield, quite often problem families.

On one memorable afternoon she and Martha drove out to the large Larkfield Estate outside Greenock, to perform a Salvation Army dedication service of the MacTaggart children. The home was poor, the five small children pale and restless because they had been ill. Yet with the quiet assurance of the doctor's presence the simple service was a meaningful one for all concerned, and Martha felt the presence of the Lord was real.

On most occasions, the doctor's car was an ordinary beast of burden, collecting and conveying people, and ferrying secondhand clothes, but at Christmas time it was transformed into a Santa Claus sleigh for the transportation of goodies and gifts in the shape of Christmas parcels for needy families.

It was unusual for Martha to get much sleep on Christmas Eve. She and Dorothy had to be up early preparing the Goodwill Centre for their usual festivities of the day. Barely had she settled down to her early morning devotions one Christmas morning at Greenock when there was a knock on the front door.

A small boy, pinched and woebegone, held out his grubby hand in which lay a few coppers. 'Me Ma says, please could you ring the Gas. We can't get nae gas, and the bairn's bad and wants a hot drink the noo . . .'

'Come away in, lad,' Martha said with a smile. 'I'll away and get my coat. Meanwhile here's a happy Christmas to you for being a good boy and running an errand for your Ma.' She led him to the big decorated Christmas tree and watched as his face lit up at the sight of the crackers and colourful silver balls. Uncertain if there was more in this plea for help than met the eye, Martha packed a few goodies and toys among her First Aid equipment and they set out.

Ian's home was down uneven, rubbish-laden stairs in a basement. Unlatching the door, Martha found herself in a large low-ceilinged room which was damp and cheerless: no fire, no light, no Christmas decorations. Martha's expert eye took in the details swiftly and she moved immediately in the gloom to the unmade bed where Ian's mother was lying. The baby whimpered and then began to scream as she approached and the mother looked helplessly round for anything that would stop it. She was obviously exhausted and the baby badly needed changing. Martha bent to look at the child, and became aware of three pairs of young eyes watching her from the other side of the bed where Ian's other brothers and sisters were huddled.

'We canna get nae gas,' the woman said weakly, 'Me man's gane a' left me — with not a thing. An' young Rory needs his feed that bad — I dinna know what to do.' She struggled to sit up and tend the baby but Martha gently pushed her back.

'Just you wait until I fix the gas. I've got the money here . . . and then we'll have some warmth and some Christmas cheer.'

She knelt in the dim corner by the meter to put in the shillings she had brought with her. But they would not go in. Turning on her torch she discovered why. The meter had been broken open and the money box ripped out. Trying not to make too much of this, she stood up and went to her bag.

'Now, what a good thing it is, to be sure, that I put a thermos of boiling water in my bag. We'll have young Rory seen to in a trice.' She managed to find the baby's feed and made it up with a measure of hot water. A clean nappy solved his other problems, and she handed him to his mother to be fed.

'Now, before I pop back to the Centre to ring the Gas people, has Father Christmas been today?'

'Nae, miss,' the wistful faces watched from the other side of the bed. It nearly broke Martha's heart to see so little effort made to brighten their day — thank God she could do something.

Giving — giving — giving. That seems to be the lot of the Goodwill Officers who are trained to offer help to all unless they are convinced they are being hoodwinked. Christian love and charity does occasionally have its limits — but these seem to be reached only seldom by such people as Martha Field.

But it worried Martha that many deserving old people never joined the weekly luncheon club — for they were too sick or frail to leave their homes. Martha was an intrepid visitor — not content to wait for requests for help to come to her. In Greenock she continued her normal custom of spending at least one day a week consistently visiting from door to door, seeking those in need.

'Find out what's behind those front doors,' she told Dorothy. 'And you'll often find people in need.'

It was true that sometimes she had to be pretty persistent and 'canny', for older people could be 'cussed' and independent, though not without reason.

Mr. and Mrs. Alexander were a couple she was told about by the local newsagent. They appeared to have turned themselves into pathetic recluses. The wife had been bedridden for six years, though this did not entirely explain why they seldom had visitors, and maintained a fiercely independent attitude refusing to let anyone into their tenement flat.

Martha's first friendly efforts were frustrated by a firm 'no admittance', from Mr. Alexander. She was nonplussed, until a friendly neighbour suggested she call on Friday afternoons, when the old man left the door unlocked while he went to do the shopping.

The Friday following, Martha made her first successful visit and remembered it particularly because it was St. Patrick's Day, March 17th. When she knocked and pushed open the door of the poorly furnished flat, she called out cheerily so that the old lady would not be frightened. Mrs. Alexander was lying in a crumpled, badly-made bed in the next room, which was bare of even the most basic small comforts. Martha introduced herself and the two women were busy chatting by the time Mr. Alexander returned. He was a little stiff at first, but once the gruffness of his manner had thawed over a cup of tea and some oatcakes which Martha had brought with her, she broached the subject of improving their living conditions, and particularly Mrs. Alexander's very limited existence.

There was a slight hesitation which puzzled her until she

realised they thought they might have to pay. She hastened to explain that with the help of funds at the Goodwill Centre, she could provide them as gifts. Why not a wireless, she suggested, Mrs. Alexander would be able to listen to that all day long?

The old lady shook her head doubtfully. Mr. Alexander looked down at his gnarled hands, clasping and unclasping them and relapsing into silence. Eventually Mrs. Alexander spoke up.

'No, we want no wireless, thank you. But I would dearly like a budgie. You'd like that wouldn't you, love? It'd be a real treat to hear it chattering and singing. That would be real companionship, that would.'

'What a good idea.' Martha agreed. As soon as she could decently excuse herself, she visited the local pet shop to see if they had a bird suitable. Maybe the fact that it was St. Patrick's Day had something to do with it, but she chose a sleek young bright green budgie, borrowed a cage until a permanent one could be bought, and carried him proudly back.

The Alexanders were ecstatic and insisted that he must be called 'Paddy' in honour of their new Irish friend and his beautiful colour. He proved to be a great success, and a genuine source of delight to both the old people. In fact Pa Alexander unbent sufficiently to admit that what he actually longed for was a gramophone.

That sounded a little more difficult to find, but Martha remembered the market. Sure enough on a secondhand stall, she and Dorothy found a big old-fashioned gramophone, complete with horn, going for only sixteen shillings. It proved to be not only a bargain but a great success — for with Paddy chatting and the gramophone playing the old people's spirits improved considerably.

Of course, over the months the two officers were keeping an eye on Mrs. Alexander's physical comforts also, with bedbaths and hairwashing sessions. When the colder weather came their visits were if anything more frequent, but they were always sure of a warm welcome now.

Then Pa Alexander arrived, very distressed at the Goodwill Centre, early one morning.

'Major, something awful has happened,' he said dolefully, pulling at his muffler in his agitation. 'Prepare yourself for a terrible shock.'

Martha drew him inside hurriedly, fearing the worst. Had Ma Alexander been taken worse, she wondered.

'You see,' he went on, drawing out a large handkerchief and wiping his dripping nose. 'The spring on the gramophone's bust. And it'll cost nine shilling to mend. And worse than that Paddy's stopped talking and Mrs. A's fretting something awful.'

Martha's sense of anti-climax was comical; she burst out laughing with relief that nothing worse had happened. A visit to the little flat soon revealed that matters were just as gloomy as Pa Alexander had said. A distinct air of listlessness hung over the silent gramophone and budgie.

Talking it over later with Dorothy, she voiced their problem. 'We just haven't the money to buy them a decent gramophone, and that's the truth of it.'

'I know, Major,' Dorothy put in. 'Why don't we appeal for one? If we tell the Home League ladies or perhaps the folk at the Corps ... With Christmas coming and all, surely ...'

'Better still, Lieutenant,' Martha interrupted. 'Let's put an advert in the paper in the "Wanted" column! With Christmas coming, folks will enter into the spirit of the thing, I'm sure.'

So an advertisement was duly placed in the *Greenock Telegraph* just before Christmas and the response was wonderful. Televisions and wireless sets in good condition were offered as well as the necessary gramophone. Mr. and Mrs. Alexander were told of all the other items, but firmly stuck to their guns. On Christmas Eve, Martha and Dorothy had the joy of calling in to deliver the 'present' of a new portable gramophone accompanied by a number of records.

The excitement was intense, for while the records were played the Christmas decorations were put up and the four of them laughed and sang. As the last record came to an end, Pa Alexander got slowly to his feet and solemnly took off the cap, which he always wore indoors or out.

'I'd like us to pray,' he said gruffly.

All heads were bowed in the silence. 'Dear God, we want to thank Thee for these joys what we have received this day, and for Major and Lieutenant and all the friends who care for us and come so regular to see us. Amen.'

With his cap restored to its rightful place, Pa Alexander switched the gramophone on again and the merriment resumed.

They seemed so different from the two lonely, depressed old people who refused to have anything to do with anyone. For Pa Alexander actually to suggest a prayer was yet another sign of the growing affection and respect he had for the two officers.

On a memorable occasion when Martha entered the home, the old man seemed unduly pleased with himself. There was a kind of undercurrent of excitement and much rubbing of hands in suppressed glee. When she had finally seen to Ma Alexander's needs, Pa bounced to his feet and said, 'Here, look, I've got a surprise for ye. Close your eyes.'

Martha sat waiting with eyes closed. Suddenly the room was full of the sound of a lively Irish jig which set her feet tapping. The tune was 'My girl is an Irish girl' and when the record was turned over the singer launched into the cheeky folk song, 'Paddy McGinty's goat' — some of the words of which Martha could remember quite well:

> 'He's eaten my bank note,' said Mickey with the hump,
> They ran for the doctor, he brought a stomach pump,
> He pumped and he pumped for that twenty dollar note,
> But all he got was ninepence out of Paddy McGinty's
> goat!'

On more than one occasion, however, the two officers failed in what they considered was their duty. They could not convince the couple that their general standard of living could be vastly improved if they applied to Social Security for financial help. Pa Alexander's tiny pension was barely able to keep the two of them warm and fed, and Martha could not understand their reluctance. Then one afternoon the old lady confessed that they didn't want to lose the budgie and the gramophone, and if the man from the National Assistance Board came, he was sure to say they must go.

Eventually Martha persuaded them to fill in the appropriate forms, reassuring them that no-one would make them part with Paddy or the gramophone. Martha made sure she was there when the man from the National Assistance Board called, to give the old couple her encouragement.

Of Paddy's cage and the gramophone there was no sign! A muffled 'cheep' alone betrayed the budgie's hidden presence somewhere in the small flat. Martha looked around surreptitiously until she located the poor bird, in the recesses of the coal bunker, his cage hidden under a cloth. She longed to rescue him, but held her peace until the visitor had gone.

Sarah and John Betts were no wealthier than the Alexanders, but they led not nearly such a quiet life. John, for one, liked his spirits and his baccy, and though he and Sarah were firm in their affection for each other, when he was drunk, which was often, he was not averse to knocking Sarah about. Sarah, despite the manhandling she received, was genuinely concerned about his welfare, especially when she fell gravely ill and guessed she was going to die. Often when one of the Salvation Army officers sat with her, she would tell them how worried she was about what would happen to John when she was gone. Her favourite hymn which they sang with her was:

'Throw out the life-line across the dark wave,
There is a brother whom someone should save;
Somebody's brother! O who then will dare
To throw out the life-line his peril to share.'

Seeking to reassure Sarah about John they promised to keep an eye on him. One way of getting to know him better was at the Friday evening men's meetings where refreshments were provided in the hopes that the men would not spend the evening and all their wages in the pub. Sadly, by the time John reached the meetings at the Goodwill Centre, he was often the worse for drink. They marvelled at Sarah's patience with him, and wondered if he really cared that she was anxious about him.

When it came to the day of Sarah's funeral, he was so drunk that he could not even follow the cortege and Martha had to have help to carry him home and put him to bed.

He promised her that he would stay there and sleep off the effects of his excesses. But being Saturday, the lure of the pub proved too much for him. Very late that night, returning to the tenement flat he tripped and fell down the stairs.

The first Martha knew about all this was on Sunday morning when the Ward Sister of the local hospital rang to tell her that a Mr. Betts was in her ward and asking for her. In his fall he had managed to get the stem of his pipe wedged in the roof of his mouth so had been brought in to casualty.

By the time Martha reached the hospital, he had already had an operation to remove the stem, and had great difficulty in speaking. Nevertheless, he did not seem very chastened by his accident, quite the opposite. He was the life and soul of the ward, considering the whole thing a huge joke — for in swallowing his pipe he reckoned he had gone one better than Rabbie Burns. He was also very impressed with the hospital and the nurses, and particularly the pair of pyjamas he had been provided with. He'd never had anything quite like them before!

Martha was relieved to see him so well. If the hospital could contain him for a few days, it would be a golden opportunity for her and Dorothy to 'do out' the flat, now that Sarah would not be there to do it for him. The place was in a dreadful state, and because of his inebriated condition, no-one else would bother with him.

On his discharge from hospital, he was sober enough to appreciate what the two officers had done and Martha gave him a firm ultimatum. Could he not try moderating his drinking a bit? She made it clear that he was welcome on Friday evenings at the Goodwill Centre, and she would always take an interest in him for Sarah's sake, but they would find it a lot easier to do so, if he would cut down on the drink. Needless to say he did try, but he found it hard to change his ways for long.

Perhaps he represents the people Dorothy Lindsay had in mind when she summed up their five year's hard work in Greenock with 'We did not see a lot of people at the Mercy Seat, but many people felt the touch of God on them through Major.'

Certainly these thoughts were echoed by the *Greenock*

Telegraph when it paid tribute to the two women, not many weeks after Dorothy Lindsay had been posted to Notting Hill Goodwill Centre in London and Martha had received her Marching Orders to go to Nottingham in May 1959.

'Many local people especially those concerned in social and welfare work, will be sorry to see the departure from our midst of Major Martha Field and Lieutenant Dorothy Lindsay,' read a surprised Martha in the paper for Friday, May 15th. Her eyes moved slowly down the column of type. 'Such has been the value of their work in the town that strenuous efforts were made by the Welfare Officer, Mr. Thomas Sutherland, and ex-Provost Gerrard, to have their transfers delayed.'

Did they, bless them? Martha was even more surprised. She read on, 'Major Field, despite the fact that her shift to Nottingham means promotion, would have been delighted to stay on in Greenock.' (That's true, she agreed inwardly.) 'But the five years the two officers have been here already, is much longer than the normal Salvation Army appointment, and headquarters ruled that the transfers must be fulfilled . . .'

Indeed the time to leave Greenock and its dockyards and the view of the Clyde from the Goodwill Centre had come. Lindsay had already left, going south to work in London and eventually to marry and emigrate to Australia. For Martha the journey south was to be a much shorter one. She had been put in charge of the Army's Goodwill and Welfare work in Nottingham, the Founder's birthplace.

Never in her wildest dreams had she seen herself serving in the Founder's city. She trembled at what was going to be expected of her. God would have to be her strength and stay in a new way in the days ahead.

One small consolation cheered her departure from Greenock however. She was thrilled to know that one of her own Sunday school children from her Belfast Corps days was coming to help with the Goodwill work, as assistant to her successor—so the Irish tradition would be upheld at Regent Street.

11

'In its own Grounds . . .'

Captain Sophie Wilson opened the letter from Martha with eager anticipation. Since her Marching Orders from headquarters had arrived at the beginning of May 1961 telling her that she was to leave Gourock to join Major Field, she had been trying to decide whether she was thrilled or terrified at the thought of going to Nottingham, the Founder's city. Little had she thought when she'd been there for an Easter campaign as a cadet that she would one day come back there to work. It had seemed a fine city to her, though she had been there only ten days admittedly . . .

'Dear Sophie,

I'm so happy to know you are coming to join me next week. We'll meet you at Nottingham Midland station at 6.00 p.m., and I'm surely looking forward to seeing you again. It seems an age since we were together at Larkfield. I'm longing to hear about all the children — and how the MacTaggarts are getting on.

I don't know quite what you'll think of our Slum Post here. It's not like Regent Street, I'm afraid. But it does stand in its own grounds . . .'

As Sophie got down to her packing she decided North Street sounded quite presentable.

Martha's warm smile and quick hug at the station exit made Sophie feel immediately welcome, though she thought she had seen her officer colleague in better spirits. Behind Martha's glasses there were dark shadows around her eyes and her skin had a pallor Sophie hadn't seen there when last they met in Greenock.

In a matter of moments Major John Jackson had stowed Sophie's case in the boot of his car and they were off on a brief guided tour of the city of Robin Hood fame. The two landmarks she had seen from the train were soon identified as Castle Rock and the Council House, the latter being Nottingham's imposing Town Hall with its pillared façade and graceful dome. Then there were glimpses of the River Trent, the University, the Trent Bridge Cricket Ground, before they began climbing a hill away from the city centre.

'This is Sneinton,' called Major Jackson. 'And there on your right is St. Stephen's Church where William Booth was christened.'

Just before they reached the church, the car turned sharply to the left. 'And there's his birthplace — Number 12 it is. Major Marshall's in charge of the museum, of course.' Sophie peered to her right again, at the house set behind trees and railings in a row of terraced dwellings. But before she was sure which was the right one, they were off up the slope, entering an area of narrow streets quite different from the ones they had just left. Ramshackle crowded buildings, many of them derelict, back-to-back alleyways with gutters running down the centre; rubbish and broken windows and unsightly lines of grey washing all contributed to the general air of damp, dirt and decay. A rat slid quickly over the doorstep of one outhouse and began nosing in the refuse spilling out of an overturned dustbin. Sophie turned away with a shudder.

The car began to slow down and drew up outside a

building standing in solitary state. 'In its own grounds' Martha had written and it was certainly true. What she had not explained to Sophie was that its grounds were the remains of a demolition site. The bulldozer had flattened any neighbours the old North Street Slum Post had ever had . . . with devastating consequences on the fabric and the future of the building. As the same 'joke' had been played on Martha when she first arrived in Nottingham, she could not resist playing it on Sophie, whose hearty chuckle she wanted very much to hear. But no chuckle came.

Sophie was in fact so shaken by what she saw she was silent. Never in all her experience had she seen a place like it. There was not even a front door step. No doorknocker either. Just a badly fitting door, its paint peeling, the wood cracking at the corners. When Martha opened it and stood back there was a dark narrow passage with bags and suit-cases lining one wall. Before Martha took her any further she suggested Sophie should dump her bags along the other 'for the time being', and led the way through a creaking door to reveal to Sophie's astonished eyes the 'kitchen', if such it could be called. All it boasted in the way of heating, lighting or cooking facilities were three paraffin lamps, on the middle one of which sat a kettle.

Sophie tried to push down her feeling of disbelief. Did the Army really expect them to live here and to run this — this slum — as a Goodwill Centre? How could they brighten other people's lives, bringing them into these ghastly circumstances?

When the candles were lit and the kettle had eventually boiled Martha apologetically explained that things had got much worse only recently. Nottingham Corporation wanted to demolish the building and while a desperate search for new premises had been going on, the Army were trying to negotiate for compensation. She hoped that before not many more months had passed they would be out of the place altogether. In the meantime she was holding meetings in people's homes and at a building they had been offered in Storer Street a few minutes' walk away.

'But it's amazing,' Martha went on cheerfully. 'People seem to like coming here. We've often held meetings by candlelight — very cosy and warm it is, and all. Then, of course, we — Slater and I — would go round and hold cottage meetings in people's homes when things got really bad here.'

Martha's cheerfulness encouraged Sophie to see the bright side of North Street — but in reality it was a grim situation and could not get much worse. There had already been one gas explosion which had sent Martha and her two assistant officers out into the dark in their night-clothes to be taken in by nearby friends for five weeks.

'To tell you the truth, Sophie,' Martha went on, 'if you didn't laugh about some of the things that happened here, you'd cry.'

But it was a fact that when Sophie joined Martha, there were probably fewer of 'her people' living near the centre in Sneinton than ever before. The demolition scheme which had so shattered North Street was part of Nottingham's drive to dispense with its unsightly and notorious slums and rehouse the population on new estates and it meant many friends and contacts were being moved away.

The Nottingham of the sixties was a city of huge contrasts: new estates, by-passes and road-widening schemes, fine city centre buildings but also deprivation, loneliness, a rising crime rate and the worst slums in Britain. A survey carried out by the Adult Education Department of Nottingham University in 1967 called St. Ann's 'a slum which crawls on over more than 300 of Nottingham's dirtiest acres' and claimed that fifty per cent of the children there were living in poverty. But even the new estates failed to eradicate desperate social needs. One such, Clifton, rehousing 30,000 of Nottingham's slum dwellers, was known to some as 'a graveyard with lights' because it was so devoid of character and recreational facilities.

Yet Nottingham had a high reputation to uphold as a busy county centre, a university city, with a weekly cattle market and the annual Goose Fair attracting thousands. Its industrial trinity of Boots, Players and Raleighs added commercial importance to its other well-known trade — lacemaking — which had gradually adapted to other requirements such as hosiery.

But there seemed to be a kind of blind spot when it came to the appalling needs of a vast number of its citizens. As one journalist on the local paper put it 'Nottingham has been calling itself the Queen of the Midlands for so long that it has often dazzled itself with the title. Under the regal robe has been swept a great deal of poverty.'

Slums apart, it was the first time for many a year that Martha had found herself in an inland city many miles from the sea. It had been hard, too, not to compare her situation with Greenock, and the 'Slum Post' there with its commanding view of the Clyde. There, she had felt part of a local community — in Nottingham, with a population four times the size and no local minister or journalist to take up the cause, she felt powerless to do anything.

So keenly did she feel, when Lt.-Colonel Jewkes visited the Council in April 1961 on her behalf, that he asked her not to 'let rip' in case she said too much!

For it was undeniable that the two years Major Field had spent at North Street before Sophie's arrival had been unspeakably grim. Never one to talk about her own problems or needs at any time, Martha said remarkably little to anyone, and resolutely refused to be moved. But there were those among her family, her friends and her senior colleagues who were concerned about the conditions under which she was working. She was no longer young, and at fifty lacked the robust health needed for the kind of life she was leading. Some were convinced that she would suffer a breakdown in health if she stuck it at North Street. Then, suddenly, some kind gesture or incident, when she could meet a desperate need, would lift her spirits.

There was her first Christmas there, for instance, brightened by the generous thought of the local shopkeeper who had to close his shop due to a sudden death in the family. He asked The Salvation Army Goodwill Centre to make use of the perishable foodstocks. So on Christmas Eve morning, Martha and her two assistants collected many pounds of sausages and family size pork pies which added a real fillip to the Christmas food parcels they were distributing.

That Christmas, also, she discovered the hidden agonies of the 'hopeless' cases who had made the slums of Sneinton their home. And found not everyone of them was hopeless. The children's Christmas party was beginning at North Street, and Martha waiting at the front door to greet the children could hear the early arrivals singing with the young men Lieutenants from the Memorial Halls, the central Corps in Nottingham. The fairy lights decorating the Queen Adelaide pub opposite winked and glowed in the growing afternoon gloom. As Martha glanced across at the building her feet stopped tapping to 'Here we go round the Mulberry bush'. A body was lying on the pavement. Closer inspection revealed it was a woman, and as Martha knelt to lift her head she realised she was very drunk. Her grey face and dishevelled appearance made her look about eighty, though in reality she was a good deal younger.

She could not move the woman on her own — but the young Lieutenant helping with the party would do. After some difficulty they managed to get the woman, who was semi-conscious, on to her feet, and asked her where she lived. Though her voice was slurred, they managed to grasp that it was Notintone Place. It was only about five minutes walk away, but with each taking an arm, Martha and the Lieutenant took fifteen to steer the woman to her one-roomed home, which was in a filthy condition.

As they entered the room, a foul smell assailed them. Martha's attempts to put on the light were fruitless for the electricity had been cut off and there was no gas. Groping in the gloom they found the end of a bed, but just as they were about to lower the woman on to it, Martha's hand touched a leg. There was a body already in the bed.

The reason for the stench became immediately apparent. The woman on the bed had not moved from it for days, possibly weeks. Unable to breathe for the unbearable smell, Martha and her helper were reduced to laying the drunken woman gently on the floor and retreating hastily to the fresh air. Glancing out of the grime-laden window, the sight of Number 12 Notintone Place gave Martha an idea.

'Look, Leff, we can't work in that room as it is at the moment. Major Marshall at Number 12 will help, I'm sure. Would you run there and see if she has some hankies or bandages we can use for face masks? Then call round at Dr. Jones in the next street and ask him to come. Here's some cash to buy some very strong disinfectant at the chemists. Be as quick as you can — there's a good lad.'

Before long, both officers managed to make face masks and with disinfectant ready they braved the nauseous conditions once again, to try and tend properly the two occupants.

The woman on the bed appeared to be more dead than alive, her emaciated body unwashed and fetid from lying so long in its own excrement. The doctor, appalled by the state of the whole room, called the ambulance immediately. But the woman was so ill she died shortly after admission to hospital.

The alcoholic, whom Martha had picked up off the street, survived — she was suffering from an excess of alcohol and physically was quite strong. She had been too drunk to help her friend to whom she had given her bed, which was now fit only for the flames. Martha was concerned because it was obvious that she could not stay in that room, and it was a great relief when she was taken into care. Soon she was a resident in a local authority old people's home where Martha visited her as regularly as she could. The drink was still a problem, but it was touching to be told by her, 'When you picked me up, duck, I knew the hands were different.'

An alcoholic who inflicted harm on herself was one matter but helpless ill-treated children were quite another. Both received Martha's care, but her deepest feelings went out to the pathetic child victims of parental neglect and cruelty which it was her unhappy lot to meet.

As she told Sophie about the conditions under which the two Wilson boys had been found the summer before, both women's eyes filled with tears. It had been holiday time when the NSPCC had found the two terrified little boys, aged five and seven, in a dank cellar where they had been locked by their father. Their clothing was in a terrible state and their general health revealed a sad neglect. It transpired that their mother was a mentally sick woman and it was only with the help of outsiders that she could cope with the boys at all.

Martha was asked to take the lads under her wing, and with the assistance of the local children's officer, they were soon adequately clothed by the welfare department with three pairs of everything. The Sunday school outing to Wicksteed Park was to take place the next week, and Martha asked if the boys could come with them. The day dawned warm and sunny and with specially prepared provisions (in case their mother couldn't cope) Martha collected the boys before the coach arrived.

She took the two boys to seats near the back of the bus and the happy, noisy band set off for a day in the country. Bowling along in the hot sunshine she happened to notice both the boys looked flushed and restless. Fearing they might be feeling travel sick she went across to suggest they undid their shirt collars and rolled up their sleeves in order to feel cooler. But when she undid the necessary buttons she found beneath the first shirt another, and beneath that — another! For some reason best known to herself, their mother had put three of everything on the boys that day! No wonder they were sweating so profusely! With Martha's help they managed to strip off the unnecessary layers and the two lads settled down to enjoy the sights.

From Greenock days Martha knew well that her new assistant loved children. But it was a little unfortunate for poor Sophie, still recovering from the move to Nottingham and North Street, that the two children Martha introduced her to first were in hospital after road accidents.

'We usually have Saturday afternoons off, Captain,' Martha said as she explained the weekend programme on Sophie's arrival. 'But I spend mine at the children's hospital. I'd like you to meet two friends of mine.'

In her hospital visitation Martha tried to seek out the lonely, uncared for patients — children or adults — who were without visitors. Arriving on one of the children's wards the Sister told her that there was one of her children in the ward. Martha looked round the big room pretty carefully before saying, 'There's none of mine here.'

'Ah yes,' said Sister. 'There's this little fellow, Mark. He's got nobody to visit him today. His brother has just died and the father has gone to the funeral and all he's been left is some soiled cigarette cards.'

Sophie's initiation in Nottingham was not complete,

however, until she had met Sister Goode and Sister Rogers at the Memorials Hall on Sunday morning. These two old ladies seemed to have won a high place in Martha's affection during the difficult months at North Street. And as the tiny frail seven-stone figure of Sister Rogers beamed up welcomingly at her, Sophie understood a little the claim Martha had made that the old lady 'was very rich concerning the things of the kingdom'. Visiting her was a pleasure and an inspiration, not least because her tiny kitchen was always spotless and shining and she was thrilled to join in a time of prayer, listen to the Bible or sing her favourite hymn:

'A wonderful Saviour is Jesus my Lord,
A wonderful Saviour to me.
He hideth my soul in the cleft of the rock
Where rivers of pleasure I see.'

Not least, Sister Rogers was faithful in her use of her small income. Each week, out of her pension, she set aside what she called 'The Lord's portion' before doing any shopping for her own needs.

One of the problems taken increasingly to the Lord in Martha's first two years in North Street, was her desperate need for new premises to continue the work. The search had begun before her appointment in 1959 and it was to be another six months after Sophie's arrival before the two women saw the grim shell of North Street for the last time.

The one redeeming feature about the last year there was the availability of the former youth centre in Storer Street. It was certainly in use part-time as a Goodwill Centre long before the official opening there in November 1961, but it had remained up till then only a daytime base.

Fortunately for all concerned the 'lean' years at North Street were followed by six 'fat' years at Storer Street. The house was ideal — detached, with its front door set between two bay windows in a sturdily built structure — and it even had a lawn at the front and side (a very unusual feature in that area!). It had two big rooms downstairs, ideal for meetings and serving lunches for older people and a kitchen beyond. Set in the heart of the St. Ann's area it was still right on the doorstep of desperately needy people. In fact Storer Street itself boasted the sleaziest of lodging houses for down and outs, and some of the worst narrow terraced housing with little plumbing, sanitation and no provision for recreation.

When the Army first took possession, the building still lacked the essentials for maintaining a regular service to the community, but with the generous help of Salvation Army friends and local voluntary organisations it was fully operational in November 1961. The official opening was carried out by the British Commissioner Edgar Grinsted, to whom the key was handed by an undoubtedly happier Lt.-Colonel Thomas Jewkes. At the front of the simple meeting room was an attractive wooden platform inscribed with the words: 'Jesus saves'. The place was shining with polish and vases of flowers brightened many corners. The chairs for the room had been provided by local Home Leagues, who had also helped to equip the kitchen.

The opening may have been a grand affair, but the children were not forgotten. One little coloured girl from the Sunday school presented Mrs. Grinsted with a bouquet, while most of the others had small Salvation Army flags to wave. It was also an occasion for the expression of thanks. Martha was thanked publicly 'on behalf of the General' for the work she had done 'during this very difficult period' and Lt.-Colonel Jewkes paid tribute in more detail to her devotion to 'her people'. Martha, for her part, made sure that the many donors and helpers who had made Storer Street possible did not go unacknowledged.

And if anything, the official opening certainly proved one thing about the centre — that it was still in the thick of Nottingham's needy area. When Martha rang the police to notify them there might be some extra traffic around the district for the opening the constable could hardly believe his ears.

'Where did you say all these posh cars are going to be?' he asked incredulously.

'Top of Storer Street,' Martha repeated. 'We thought we ought to have a policeman in case the traffic gets bad.'

The constable thought differently. He knew Storer Street was a notorious district for petty thieving and vandalism. Few cars parked there were left unmolested. He didn't just send one policeman, he sent four! Though as far as we know, on this occasion they were not needed!

12

All in a Day's Work

Major Martha Field bent to pick up the grubby folded piece of paper with a sinking heart. It had been pushed through the letterbox of the Storer Street Goodwill Centre, and she knew even before she read the illiterate scrawl, where it came from.

'Please bring custad in, Harrys bad, Room 5.'

Trying not to show her sense of dread to her assistant officer Captain Sophie Wilson, who was washing up after lunch, she busied herself making the egg custard.

Then she put on an overall as a precaution against having to buy another new uniform. She'd learnt her lesson the hard way, when she had popped across the way with some fresh scones for a sick man, not bothering to put on an overall. The man seemed to be wasting away without food or fluid so she lifted him up to give him a drink of water when, without any warning, he was violently sick all over her. The doctor was horrified. She must burn her uniform, he insisted, and that meant buying a new one.

'Captain, I'm just off across the way to see old Harry,' she called as casually as possible. 'Mind now, if I don't come back you're not to come in to that place on your own. You ring one of the men to come in with you. It's Room Number 5 you'll be wanting . . .'

The familiar smells greeted her as she stumbled on the uneven bare floorboards — a musty mixture of tobacco, alcohol, meths and other fumes, chiefly stale sweat and urine emanating from the totally inadequate toilet facilities in the house, and the unwashed bodies of the fifty-two residents.

Her hand faltered as she went to knock on the door of Room Number 5, for she never knew what she would find. Four or five men were crammed into each room paying £1 a week sometimes for a bed, sometimes for floor space and little else. The rooms were scarcely furnished, the house decrepit and neglected. The men, even though they were alcoholics and vagrants, deserved better than the indescribable squalor which surrounded them.

Martha pushed open the door, calling Harry's name. Filthy windows let in a minimum of light and as usual there was no light bulb in the socket. She called again and a husky moan from the corner bed gave her some sense of direction. Picking her way across the uncarpeted floor, she stepped over the slumped figure of one man, a bottle of meths under his arm. The other occupants appeared to be out, much to her relief, for it had not been unknown for her to find a man lying there with no clothes on.

As she reached Harry's side she tried to keep a firm grip on the wave of nausea which threatened to swamp her. The stench was terrible. He had been sick several times and no-one had been near him. The dirty floor was the only place for her bag and she had to balance the egg custard on her knee as she unfolded the towel. As she wiped his face and hands his eyes opened and focused on the dish. Clawlike hands reached up to grasp it and the spoon was soon put to good use.

When he had finished she asked if there was anything else he needed. He assured her that he was fine, though his bronchial wheeze and cough worried her. She knew only too well that bronchitis in these insanitary conditions, coupled with the inroads the meths had already taken on his emaciated body, could prove fatal, and it was more than her life's worth to get him into hospital, for he would lose his bed.

As she guessed, Harry refused any idea of being treated by a doctor. But there was something bothering him. As she went to get up, his hand came up and clutched hers.

'Will you put on the light. We've no light.'

'But what can I do?' Martha asked. 'I can't get the electricity switched on.'

'No, it's your light I mean. It shines in the window and when I sees the light I know yer there — and it's a comfort.'

'Oh that's fine, dearie. I'll be sure to put it on then,' Martha assured him, thinking how pathetically small one outside light seemed in comparison with the cramped squalor of that house.

Sophie Wilson looked up with a smile of relief when Martha returned. She sensed that it cost her C.O. quite a lot to go into the lodging houses, though she said little. 'If I can just get through this' was her usual plea.

'But I'm afraid, Captain,' Martha said, as she finished scrubbing herself. 'Harry should really be in hospital. But you know what'll happen if I suggest it. "What'll happen to my bed? Marco the landlord, will fill it up." They're all terrified that if they go into hospital they'll never get back. And they're right of course. Marco will fill it up as sure, as sure.'

Marco's lodging houses were only one of the desperate social problems that Martha found literally 'on her doorstep' at Storer Street. And it was not just in the rooms of the lodging houses that she met with ghastly living conditions. In the slum hovels of the area many of the less fortunate — the homeless, the drifters, the unwanted, the inadequate — had been washed up by the tide of life.

Her heart was most touched by the children, trapped within this city slum ghetto, unable to play in the freedom of sunlight and blue sky. Their only playground was the rubbish-laden alleyways and streets. It was not surprising to her, that the stress of life within these conditions forced many into petty crime or vandalism — or their parents to the end of their tether. She tried to do all she could to improve matters.

So, a typically hectic day for Martha began as she tidied her uniform, gathered up her bag and set off via Mrs. Hamilton's place, for she knew the old lady had not been well. At the top of a dark shabby staircase in a tiny room, she found Mrs. Hamilton in bed. Her heavy breathing revealed bronchitis — but Martha was glad to hear that the doctor had been. Remaking the bed quickly, Martha made sure Mrs. Hamilton was warm enough and assured her that her lunch would be brought from the Centre, before setting out for the juvenile court.

Waiting at the court for the case to come up was trying, but Martha felt that Tony, a thirteen-year-old, deserved another chance, which he might get if she put in a word for him. Indeed, when the magistrate had listened to all she had to say on the boy's behalf, he thanked her sincerely for her help.

The mouthwatering aroma of hot soup greeted Martha as soon as she opened thc door of the Centre on her return. The hush in the dining-room told her that grace had been said and everyone was tucking in to the hot lunch which was the highlight of the week for forty old-age pensioners. Once the lunch was served, she and Sophie had the chance to chat to the people and make sure that Mrs. Hamilton, and other absentees, had been taken their meal. It was essential that they clear up quickly, because the afternoon was going to take some organisation.

Mrs. Jones, who had just had her eighth child in

hospital, was due home but she was in some distress because she had no husband or family to welcome her or support her in the weeks ahead. It was the task of the two officers to do what they could that afternoon to lighten her burden.

While Martha set off for the hospital, Sophie went to Mrs. Jones' home to make the place clean and warm and prepare a meal and fresh flowers. The only minor problem occurred at the maternity hospital, owing to the lack of a suitcase for Mrs. Jones few belongings. That was soon overcome by tying all her things in a bundle, and, with baby wrapped snugly in a blanket, the homecoming was a happy one.

By the time the two officers left Mrs. Jones, it was late afternoon and the schoolchildren were running home. Almost immediately they were surrounded by youngsters, hanging on their arms, chattering, laughing and calling out. They were Martha's 'bees'. She often said she only had to turn on the outside light and open the Storer Street door for the Joy Hour and the children came 'like bees round a honeypot'.

But many of her 'bees' had sad tales to tell. As she looked round a number represented case histories where neglect had robbed the faces of childish innocence, and rosiness. There was Patsy, the little girl whose toys had to be kept at the Centre because her mother pawned them, and Colin, whose bruised body and hand-me-down clothes always made her wince.

It was time for the children's club when they reached Storer Street. Plenty of laughter and singing, games and competitions, kept everyone busy before the brief epilogue. Then Martha and Sophie could spare a few moments for a wash and brush up and a cup of tea, before the adult meeting followed. The day had been a busy one and the two officers were pretty tired when they eventually shut the front door on the last visitor, wondering if any of their actions had made someone think seriously about the claims of Christ upon their lives.

Certainly events later that year revealed that, however busy or typical that day had been, some people were glad to come to the Army for more than material help. The luncheon club, for instance, seemed routine enough. Yet, for two elderly people, it was the place where they found romance and they wanted the Army to ask God's blessing on the wedding that was in the offing. Mavis was a widow who had moved into a new council flat not very far from the Centre and had been attending the meetings and lunches for some time. John, a widower, was someone Martha had invited in on the spur of the moment when she met him in the icy streets at Christmas. When John and Mavis got chatting, they discovered they had both been born in Sheffield and had been childhood sweethearts.

Martha had jokingly said at some point to the club, 'I'll do the reception here for the first pair of you to get married.' April 1962 and she was doing just that for Mavis and John, after their wedding at the William Booth Memorial Halls in the city centre. It was a very happy occasion, not least for John, though Martha had a hard job beforehand, persuading him that he could not possibly wear his old khaki to go up the aisle!

'I thought I'd give you all a treat,' John explained.

'You'll give us no treat!' Martha said indignantly. 'You get yourself a decent jacket to wear.'

On the great day, there was John resplendent in blue serge bought for nine shillings from the secondhand shop down the road. A week later the jacket was back in the shop and the nine shillings was back in John's pocket! But there was little doubt that John was much happier. He had been so lonely in his cheerless one room that he had caught himself talking to the wall. Now he shared Mavis's bright modern flat and neither of them was lonely any longer.

And what of the children who came to the weekly meetings whom Martha and Sophie loved and taught and played with and prayed over? There was no greater reward for the two officers than to see them enjoying themselves at camp — the undoubted climax of the year's work. A week spent in the country camping at Willoughby on the Wolds, south-west of Nottingham, meant getting the children away from the grime and garbage of the grey streets and into the green fields for perhaps the first time in their lives.

Many happy stories abound about this yearly treat, though it was not all fun. A tremendous amount of hard work went into preparing, packing and transporting the children (boys with Sophie in the furniture van, girls with Martha on the bus), then setting up the camp itself — unloading the van, erecting the tent and cooking for and entertaining thirty children, many of whom were not little angels.

The first year she took them to camp, in the summer of 1959, Martha was afraid that they would disgrace her in some way. Here was this quiet sleepy Midland village invaded by tough youngsters, many of whom had known little else but the street urchin's code of 'snatch and run' or 'finder's keepers'.

On arrival at the farm, where they had the use of a large field with a hut for eating, (and sleeping the girls) Martha looked around in trepidation. Since her hopfield days she had not been to camp and many things were new to her. But one thing was imperative, she and her helpers must put up the tent for the boys to sleep in and make the hungry youngsters something to eat. She shooed the children out of the hut and told them to play in the fresh air until she called them.

It was no more than five minutes before one lad came

back. 'Ere Major, can I have a bowl? There's hundreds and thousands of apples on them trees over there . . .'

'No, you cannot have a bowl and Jim—you're *not* to pick any of the fruit. It belongs to the farmer, not us!' Martha could tell by the disbelieving expression on his face that it was not going to be easy to get the children to understand they could not help themselves. She read them the riot act over tea.

'You are not to pick the farmer's apples under any circumstances. Do you hear? If you want any apples, you come to me or Captain for them!'

From the meal table a boy's voice called back, 'An if yer wants any plums, yer can come ta me fur 'em.'

But there was often a touch of pathos in incidents that happened at camp. For the deprivations suffered by some children were revealed more starkly. There was the small boy who explained his lack of nightclothes with 'Only boys who win the Duke of Edinburgh's Award wear pyjamas.' Or the first night when Martha checked the girls to find eight small children from two families, who had found settling down in separate beds for the first time too daunting, had pulled their camp beds together and fallen asleep holding hands. Perhaps most heartrending of all was the little lad whose mother was a prostitute and whose 'uncle' beat him. His poorly clad, undernourished and bruised body, began to swell and his skin developed a rash at camp, simply because he was not used to good plain food.

The doctor who treated him for this, was so concerned that he wanted to take him into his own home to help him recover. But the little boy refused to go, frightened he'd miss camp. And there was Stewart, whose father was in prison for neglecting him, crying in his sleep with the pain of a festering, untended sore on his hand which he was terrified to show to Major, for fear she would send him home.

Conversely, the positive joy of camp — which was pretty primitive by any standards — was to see the children tucking into three big meals a day and growing rosy and chubby in the sunshine. Martha reckoned she and her assistants cooked something like a hundred meals a day on small oil stoves, the only other facility on the site being running cold water. The food they cooked was provided with the help of friends — meat from a butcher in Nottingham, dairy produce and fruit from the farmer and the cost of the whole week met by money given by Nottingham businessmen.

The village community not surprisingly wondered quite what had hit them during the week. Some mums kept their children indoors and the lady in the village shop dreaded their arrival; besieged by thirty small children all wanting sweets, bubble gum, ice creams, crisps and pop, all at once, it was a wonder she could cope. The vicar of the parish church, trying to adjust to the invasion of his tiny congregation by thirty fairly lively youngsters, was startled by one little girl leaping to her feet when she heard him saying how everybody, even dustmen, could play their part in helping the community. 'Don't you dare say anything against the dustbin men,' she shouted. 'My dad's a dustman!' but if there were complaints, there were happily those in Willoughby on the Wolds who welcomed them each year.

Camp could also be guaranteed to produce the unexpected. For all their naughtiness, some of the children did grasp the fact that Major and Captain did not take them away, just to watch their thin bodies growing plump and brown; although that obviously gave them great pleasure.

If she wanted encouragement, Martha could forget the high jinks of the naughtier children, and remember the progress of some of the older ones she took to camp. Tony, for instance, was a skinny redheaded lad from a poor home, whom she had often mothered in Nottingham. At his first camp, she had had to wash him and provide clothes for him, glad to see his massive appetite satisfied by the three meals a day and his thin frame filling out a little.

Over the years he continued to come with her, until he was old enough to be a helper. She asked him to censor the postcards the children sent home and had smiled when he was appalled by the blasphemous words used by little ones half his age. Most of them knew no better, having heard the language used all the time at home. Often if Tony could not come full-time he would gladly travel down from Nottingham for the day. For camp had come to mean a great deal to him. Brigadier Gladys Taylor, who helped Martha at the camp most years, heard Tony say as he was leaving one evening, 'Thank you, Major, for all you've done for me.'

'He must have enjoyed himself today to say that,' Gladys said.

'Oh yes, I'm sure he did,' Martha replied, 'but he wasn't just thanking me for today only. He remembers being a small skinny boy just like some of these lads here. And he remembers how he was helped to get out of that and get on.'

Tony did get on. His contact with the loving faith of the Salvation Army officers at camp and at home, brought him to a living faith of his own and he became a Salvationist. Meanwhile he worked hard at his schooling, and won a place at Hull University. Quite an achievement for a lad from a working class home in the back streets of Nottingham!

The lads who led Sophie such a dance at camp were not so good back at Storer Street either. But, once again, there were surprises. Self Denial Week, after they moved to the new Centre, was a case in point. Martha had announced the week's appeal to the young people's group and was taken aback when the boys came to her afterwards. 'Look, don't you worry, Major, about raising money that is. Because we can always do a few telephone boxes down the bottom of the street there and get you some cash.'

She explained carefully why that was not her idea of Self Denial or raising money — and suggested a few more legitimate methods. The next Sunday, when she gave the appeal she had her qualms when one of the same boys came forward with a paperbag full of coppers.

'Wherever did you get all those from?' she asked, relieved to hear him explain: 'Well you see, Major, I've been collecting empty beer bottles and getting the money back on them.'

13

The Day's Work Never Done

'Sally, what have you got there?' asked a puzzled Martha.

In the bitter winter weather of 1963 she had gone to open the front door of Storer Street Goodwill Centre early, so that the children would not have to wait outside in the cold for Sunday school to begin. As usual the wood-panelled Hall was shining with polish and the loving care lavished on it by the cleaner, and the sight of two of the children depositing what looked like bags of food on the spotless surface of the sideboard at the back caused her some concern.

In answer to her question, Sally explained, 'It's bread and real butter, Major. It's for Stewart and Patsy. You see, they don't get much at home and they're always hungry — especially on Saturdays and Sundays.'

Martha tried to recall Patsy and Stewart, and remembered how frail they looked. A few inquiries soon confirmed the children's story. The house where they lived was a shambles and the mother of the two children, pregnant. She was not able, at the best of times, to devote much care and attention to them, and they were in desperate need.

Unwashed, often barely clad in the bitterest of weathers, and invariably unfed, Martha's task was first and foremost to see that they had the essentials. She lost count of the times she washed their filthy uncared-for bodies and exchanged their torn clothes for better ones from the secondhand clothes cupboard, and, of course, she made it her duty (and not the Sunday school children's) to see that they were adequately fed each time an opportunity arose. Her heart went out to these two unfortunate bairns in a particular way, and whenever she could, she hugged and 'loved' them, giving them the affection which their own mother often failed to give. Their drawn faces would break into joyful smiles when she took time to play with them, and it was pitiful to discover that the toys they provided for the children, if taken home, mysteriously 'disappeared'. They had been sold to raise money for the mother's own needs — beer, cigarettes, make-up — not the children's. It never occurred to the mother that the children would benefit from a day out. The first time Stewart went with Martha to camp, he looked around wonderingly. 'Where's all the sky come from? And where's all the chimney pots gone?'

In caring for the children, Martha also did what she could to help their mother, Mrs. Robinson. When the time for the new baby's arrival drew near she managed to provide a secondhand pram, but, improving their living conditions was far more difficult. The upstairs rooms of the house were unfit for habitation with a leaking roof, rotting plaster and a general air of total neglect. Downstairs, the mother and children lived in two rooms, their furniture consisting of a bed, a chair and a television set. The 'man of the house' never seemed to be there for long and did absolutely nothing when he was. When he was not there, a succession of 'uncles' did not appear to take an interest in the place either.

The bitter winter weather of 1963 in which Martha first met Patsy and Stewart, continued to hold Britain in its icy grip. Soon the Goodwill Centre was in growing demand as the elderly and the sick — as well as many others — called on them for help. Their selfless devoted care over the nine-week cold spell provided a headline in the local evening paper: 'City Ice Age Heroines Worked 20-Hour Day'.

'In many ways it was just like the blitz,' Martha was quoted as saying — and a glance at the lengthy four-column report reveals why. It begins: 'A salute today to two fresh-faced heroines of Nottingham's ice age — Major Martha Field and Captain Sophie Wilson of The Salvation Army. They worked far beyond the call of reasonable duty to aid the old, the poor, needy and underprivileged who faced real and severe hardships from the bitterest weather anyone can remember. Day after day, relentlessly throughout the harsh spell they have been out and about for nineteen or twenty hours out of twenty-four. The period since Christmas presented an exceptional challenge. They met it nobly, for they slithered and slid around the city with their vacuum flasks of hot soup; went round early in the mornings lighting fires and making cups of tea at the homes of the elderly and infirm; cooked 295 hot dinners served at the Goodwill Centre, or rushed round to the bedridden; distributed blankets and warm clothing to those in need; went round late at night to tuck people into bed and serve them with hot drinks; and scores of other jobs as well — organising water at homes where all pipes were frozen ...' The list goes on and on; 118 children and adults received warm clothing and shoes; 226 toys, 105 food parcels, and a pram plus pram bedding were distributed. A fleet of cars from the Canadian Air base outside the city arrived bringing airmen and food parcels to aid their work and the human often humorous incidents livened up the proceedings. The paper recorded two of these: the old lady who refused the offer of a rubber hot-water bottle with 'I don't want anything to do with those newfangled things!' and the one who sipped Martha's hot soup and said: 'Ah, you can't beat a nice drop of stout in this weather!' The concluding sentence commented: 'There is no material reward for what these women do, but they are among the happiest I have met. "It is a joy to serve," they say.'

Someone, and it was certainly not Martha, sent this report to National Headquarters, for she received a letter from the British Commissioner Edgar Grinsted saying: 'I commend you on all the devoted service you and the Captain have rendered during the cold spell . . . I have read the report in the *Evening News* with interest.' And the March 9th issue of *The War Cry* drew attention in a news item to the 'Ice Age Heroines' tribute also.

It was a surprise topical bonus for *The War Cry*'s editor, who had been running a fortnightly series on Martha's work in Nottingham under the title 'God in the Welfare State'. The writer had spent some time at the Storer Street Goodwill Centre, visiting with Martha and talking to her and Sophie.

He chose for his four articles particularly telling examples of the kind of people and the sort of need the Goodwill officers were seeking to help, introducing his first contribution with a reminder that Nottingham, the Founder's City, had still the desperate social needs of Booth's day: 'Modern building estates have replaced the slummy dwellings of his time; narrow cobbled streets have given way to broad by-passes, covered markets and towering office blocks; the murkiness of smelly gas lamps, a convenient cover for human misery and squalor, has been lost in the blaze of high-powered street lighting.

'But if General Booth came back today he would find the same devilish influences, the same indifference to human dignity and need. In all parts of the city — sometimes in the most surprising places — he would be incensed at the plight of little people being pushed around by the big impersonal world about them. And he would find still plenty of back streets where sin takes the light from children's eyes, where domestic brutality hides behind the cowered silence of frightened wives, and where poverty and suffering are camouflaged by suburban respectability.

'Our first call,' he went on, 'was at the home of a sixty-two-year-old woman, a house which looked from the outside like any one of the other houses in the pleasant district. The woman, covered with vermin-infested rags, was lying on a dirty mattress. Her back was partly eaten away with disease, long concealed and neglected. The stench was unbelievable. A few days before, a social worker had entered the room, gone outside to vomit and refused to return.' He goes on to record the pathetic way the woman resisted all Martha's attempts to get her into hospital, though happily she did eventually succeed. The writer's second visit was to the lodging houses around Storer Street where he saw Martha's devoted care for a dying alcoholic who, like Harry, was too frightened to go into hospital because he would lose his bed. For him 'life itself had become a hateful barrier to the haven of death,' Ian McColl wrote. 'If there was an existence beyond the grave, he argued, it was certain to improve his lot; it could not be otherwise . . . His wish to die was fulfilled much sooner than he or Major Field realised. She tucked him up one night, thinking that he had passed the crisis and was on the mend. But when she returned early the next morning his bed was empty. The old man was already in the mortuary, a corpse without a mourner, unclaimed, unwanted and waiting for the formalities of a pauper's funeral. Only the Salvation Army officer was present to lament his passing.'

The third article was a retelling of one of Martha's earlier 'cases' — the drunk woman she had picked up in the street in her first year at North Street. The fourth and last, which was also perhaps the most revealing, was about a visit to a lonely eighty-eight-year-old man in an isolated bungalow, who lived surrounded by pets and pet food and the most appalling squalor. His only visitors seemed to be the Goodwill Officers: 'The room, an affront to human dignity, reeked of decay; the walls were peeling, the ceiling and floor collapsing; two easy chairs one of them burst open, were worn beyond comfort, the curtains hung like dirty motheaten rags . . . Round the back of the bungalow was a mountain of empty dog meat tins, a monument to the old man's kindly heart.' And the reason why all Martha's attempts to move him had failed? He did not want to part with his four cats and his dog.

The dreadful conditions at North Street had prevented Martha from accommodating needy people as she had done in Greenock. Once they were settled in Storer Street, all that was changed.

Though she was not an 'official' prison visitor as she had been in Greenock, she still saw a good deal of the Nottingham Salvation Army Prison officer, Brigadier Head, and many of the girls who came to stay with them were on probation or parole.

At Storer Street their presence was well known to the local police and welfare officers and the constables on the Storer Street 'beat' knew that they could call on the officers' help at any time. All they had to do at night was to come to the back of the house and shine their torch on to the ceiling of Martha's bedroom and she would awake. She was such a light sleeper—she managed to be immediately alert on rising. Sometimes Sophie would wake in the morning to find guests at the breakfast table or her C.O. with a new tale of adventure to tell. On other occasions, the emergency might demand the attendance of both officers and Martha would wake her.

During her years in Nottingham Martha was increasingly conscious, possibly more than anywhere else, of the help many good friends gave to the Goodwill work. From the start she had had a stalwart part-time helper, Maud Leaper, a Nottingham Salvationist who had trained for officership. Held back by ill health, she now devoted her spare moments to the Goodwill work instead. Providing fresh flowers for the meeting hall was her special treat each week, but she also helped with the children's work, serving faithfully with the officers at the Centre for some forty years.

Many other people gave Martha part-time help, but for the first time in Nottingham she had full-time help also from local people. She met Arch and Irene Bamford in 1963. They were a married couple in their forties who had been converted while attending the William Booth Memorial Halls. After they had become Salvationists their Commanding Officer, recognising their desire to do something practical in the way of Christian service, introduced them to Storer Street and its two Goodwill Officers.

Arch was immediately struck by the cheerful dedication of their Irish/Scots partnership, and by the amount of time — not to mention energy — they seemed to expend on just getting from A to B. Neither woman could drive and the centre had no car, so it was bus or 'shank's pony'. As many of Martha's people had been rehoused on outlying estates, her journey could take anything up to an hour or two from Storer Street. Arch offered to drive the officers, whenever possible, outside his working hours, little realising quite what he had taken on — or how soon his 'working hours' were to come to an end.

Early one Sunday morning the Bamford's telephone rang.

'It's Martha Field here, I was just wondering, do you remember offering to drive me if I needed you? Well, it so happens I've got to get to Woodborough Road and there's no bus . . . Do you think you would be taking me there?'

Arch agreed immediately and picking up his Army hat, in case he managed to get to the morning meeting at the Memorial Halls, he set off for Storer Street to collect Martha, unaware that he wasn't quite dressed for the part he was to play. Once in the car Martha explained the urgency of their task. An old man had not been seen by his neighbours for some days and he was in poor health. The matter couldn't be left until the next day.

There was no reply when they reached the house, but the front door was unlatched. Martha pushed it open, calling as she did so. There was an eerie stillness but no reply. Shouting again she and Arch looked into the small dingy downstairs rooms. Nobody answered. A musty cold, unused air hung over everything.

As they reached the foot of the narrow staircase, Martha paused. 'Wish I had an overall for you. Have you a strong stomach, Arch? You never know quite what you are going to find when you come out on this sort of case.' Arch said he thought he'd be OK, as he'd served in the Forces.

'Well, I just warn you, that's all,' Martha continued as they climbed the stairs. 'You may surprise yourself . . . I've known experienced Goodwill Officers taken suddenly sick by some of the things they've been confronted with.'

They had reached the top of the stairs by this time and Martha called out again. A faint voice answered. Entering the bedroom, a terrible smell met them and Martha retreated immediately. Arch began to have an inkling why she had taken such trouble to warn him. A large handkerchief soaked in disinfectant was shoved into his hand and he followed Martha's example by tying it around his mouth and nostrils. Only then was he allowed to follow her into the room.

Martha moved quickly to the bed, but kept an eye on Arch as she did so. Then, with her large bag opened, she turned all her attention to tending the very sick and neglected old man, and his cancerous body.

Arch, whose stomach was not feeling quite as calm as he would have liked, hastened to help her lift the old man. That done, he kept his arm firmly round the patient's shoulders while Martha fed him from her flask of hot soup. Once or twice he let his eyes stray round the incredibly filthy room, for there was something out of place. Amidst the rubbish and dirt, leaning against the wall in the corner was a set of garden tools gleaming and shining, as if the old man had cleaned them that day. The man's bedclothes seemed to consist of little else than sacks and two old overcoats, and the only furniture in the room was the bed and a chair, so the man's care for his tools compared with his neglect of himself seemed strange — until Arch discovered he had been a gardener by trade.

The soup finished, Martha left Arch trying to chat with the old man about his tools and his job, and returned with a bowl of hot water. They set about the unsavoury task of undressing him together, Martha washing his limbs while Arch supported him. To Arch's amazement, all the essentials — towel, flannel, soap, toothpaste — all appeared as if by magic out of Martha's bag. Then to crown everything, even a clean vest and a pair of pyjamas were produced.

Bert, as they discovered the old man was called, still looked very frail but so much cleaner and happier, even attempting to joke feebly with his two helpers. Before they left Martha reassured Bert that she would try to get him into hospital.

As soon as they entered the Goodwill Centre, Martha insisted on Arch having a good 'scrub up' and a quick cup of tea, while she sponged his uniform. Then she was on the telephone, attempting to get Bert moved to hospital. It took a fair number of calls and a lot of persistence, but in the end she succeeded in getting the Geriatric Hospital to take him. She and Arch smiled with relief that Bert's lonely ordeal was nearly over. Before he left Storer Street Martha had ascertained that Arch and Irene would visit the old man in hospital.

It was the Bamford's first experience of hospital visitation, and proved an eye-opener to them both. Bert was not the only patient who had no family or friends to care about or visit them. If Bert's appreciation of their regular calls before his death a fortnight later were anything to go by, then there was one way in which they could serve others in the name of Christ. It was a service that they were to continue for many years.

That might have been all there was to tell. But a week or so after Bert's death, Arch lost his job. It was a shattering blow, not only shaking his self-respect but also his new-found faith. With the support of his Corps officer, and with Irene's encouragement, he determined not to sit around moping. He volunteered to help at the Goodwill Centre, while looking for work, and everyday he found himself drawn deeper into a varied and increasingly busy round of activities as Christmas drew near.

He couldn't believe that the pace could get more hectic. He watched the infinite care and energy the two officers put into preparing for Christmas, collecting toys, sorting them into age ranges, mending any that were broken, wrapping and labelling accordingly ready for the distribution, then storing up all the food and sweets for weeks beforehand, organising the parcels of groceries so that the right items were in each. 'No good sending Granny Miller a tin of baby food when what she really wants is some humbugs' . . . 'Make sure Mrs Stevens gets some honey, she loves that' . . . Where all the food came from and how it was to get to people in time, he just did not know.

Christmas Eve proved to be the grand climax of weeks of work. Many people had helped to give out parcels, but on this bitterly cold evening, Arch and his eldest son were to be Santa Claus' sleigh for the night, with Martha guiding them as they drove. They were not allowed to start until they had prayed for God's guidance and blessing and Martha had marked which parcels were to be delivered after the pubs had closed. It had not been unknown in other years, she explained, for food to be sold by the parents to buy drink.

Having delivered all but one parcel, Arch was beginning to think perhaps they'd turn home. The time was well after midnight and the driving was not helped by icy roads and freezing fog. But Martha insisted they make this last journey to a northern outskirt of the city. There was no street lighting when they arrived and most of the houses were in darkness. Martha's knock was promptly answered by a mother surrounded by her children, and Arch heard her say with a tremble in her voice. 'There now. Didn't I say the Army wouldn't let us down?'

The Bamfords also shared in the preparations for Christmas Day itself, and that was yet another revelation. Never had Arch and Irene seen such mountains of potatoes and vegetables needing to be cleaned and prepared! Christmas lunch was not just for the able-bodied who could get to the Centre, Major was also organising a 'meals on wheels' service for those who were house-bound or ill. Once again Arch enjoyed using the car to deliver some of these, able to see the joy that their visits gave, chatting with their 'customers', pulling a cracker with some, sharing a joke or a sweet with others, and usually listening to some glowing tribute to Major and Captain into the bargain.

It struck the Bamfords pretty forcibly that both women seemed overworked but rejoicing. Often very physically tired, they let little get in the way of their busy routine. So it meant a lot to them that Martha's concern for people included them also. Invariably, at the end of a hectic day,

Arch and Irene would find themselves sitting in the quarters upstairs at Storer Street, sharing a snack or a cup of tea with Martha and Sophie, and the conversation would turn to spiritual matters. As 'young' believers they had many questions about Christianity in general, and The Salvation Army in particular, and Martha never seemed too tired to explain some point that was puzzling them about Bible teaching or Army doctrine.

It was through Martha they met Mrs. Robinson, Patsy, Stewart and the new baby. Things were no better in that home, despite all the help the family were receiving, and the children's well-being in that unhealthy sordid place was still one of Martha's chief concerns. Mrs. Robinson, however, had got the message that The Salvation Army were trying to help, though the casual way she would dump Patsy and Stewart on the doorstep of Storer Street, left a lot to be desired.

Martha asked Arch and Irene if they would allow the two children to share Christmas 1964 with them, and it was arranged that Arch should pick up the children from their home. On the day itself Arch knocked at the door and introduced himself to Mrs. Robinson, whom he had never met before. He said he was the person who was to have Patsy and Stewart for Christmas. Without checking his credentials, Mrs. Robinson packed the two children into his car and waved them goodbye, not the slightest bit worried that they were in the keeping of a total stranger.

The two children were thrilled to be in a car and bounced up and down looking out of the back windows. Arch, meanwhile, had to open the front ones because of the over-powering odour of unwashed bodies behind him. A bath certainly seemed essential, even though Patsy kept insisting that she had had her hair washed specially for her holiday. Irene gently persisted, rewarded by the dirt which rolled out when she applied the shampoo. Bathtime became quite a ritual and Patsy remarked wonderingly, 'I'll shine like an angel by the time you've done.' Then added wistfully, 'Only angels don't live where I live . . .' Irene tried to reassure her they did, her heart touched by the little girl's realism.

Martha had warned Irene that the Robinsons would have little in the way of clothing when they arrived. She was not exaggerating. Despite the cold winter weather, both children lacked any warm winter underwear or night-clothes. Cotton trousers and frocks were no protection against the low temperatures, and Irene gladly supplied the missing items. On their first evening the biggest thrill — after their new nightclothes — were the slippers she had bought for them . . . something they had never owned before. They insisted on going to bed in them! They had never seen toothbrushes or paste before either and knew little about personal cleanliness.

Like her biblical namesake, Martha could never be idle for long, if she saw a need which she felt could be met. Though she had a thriving work among young people, the mums, and the old age pensioners, she managed to find yet another area where something could be done. This time it was the older men — many of whom drifted off to the pubs for company when they were lonely. With Arch Bamford on the scene it seemed an ideal time to start a men's club. She would set it up if he would run it. So it was agreed. Every Monday evening a room at the Centre was set aside for the men to play darts, billiards or other games, have refreshments, and generally enjoy a chat and make friends. At the end of the evening Martha and Sophie came in for the brief epilogue.

Martha still visited the children's hospital regularly and any children who lacked visitors, or were in any kind of trouble. She was well known to the staff too.

Just before Christmas 1964 the Ward Sister rang and

asked her to investigate the home situation of one very badly burnt little girl, whose life was in danger and who lacked any visitors.

Susan was duly visited, and Martha sang carols and chatted with her . . . discovering in the process that her mummy had left home, and daddy was ill. There were six brothers or sisters as far as Martha could make out. It sounded like an urgent case if Christmas was to mean anything for this sadly shattered family.

With the help of a Salvationist with a car (for Arch was back at work by this time) Martha was able to transport food and presents to the address the Sister had given her. It was one of the newer estates and the drive was a cold one. Neither woman was quite prepared for the sight that greeted them. Downstairs in the front room of the house huddled thirteen — not six — children in front of an empty fireplace, with their coats on to keep warm. Upstairs, the father lay ill. After the immediate needs were seen to — warmth and food and First Aid — a few questions elucidated that seven children were from next door. They had been deserted by their mother. It was indeed a tragic situation and Martha and her helper wondered how best to share out the toys they had brought for six children. In the end, after telling them the Christmas story and singing some carols Martha promised to return with some more goodies especially for Lucy, the youngest and most woebegone of all, who badly wanted a new dolly from Father Christmas.

It was sleeting heavily by the time they left the house, but Martha felt they could not let the children down. They returned in a blinding snowstorm, to give Lucy her doll. Martha was glad they had made the effort. A few weeks later Lucy was to die a tragic death.

14

A Year to Remember

1965 was for anyone remotely concerned with The Salvation Army a year to remember, for it was the centenary of the founding of William Booth's 'Christian Mission' (as the Army was first called). Throughout the year around the world, various events commemorated the occasion. Its climax in June was the Centenary Thanksgiving Service in the Royal Albert Hall, London, attended by Her Majesty Queen Elizabeth II, who said 'The Army has never failed to care for the bodies as well as the souls of men and women, however poor, however remote . . . We pray that the great work of The Salvation Army may grow and prosper in the years to come.'

For Martha in Nottingham, deeply involved as she was in her work of caring for men's souls as well as their bodies, 1965 was in some ways a pivotal year. Several significant events took place which were to influence the future course of her career.

The year began amidst national mourning for the passing of Sir Winston Churchill, but two incidents soon brightened the horizon. One was the news that Lieutenant Barnard was to join them to assist in the work and then a surprise monetary gift added further joy. Martha, in fact, misread the cheque at first sight, handing it to Sophie saying, 'Oh isn't that good? Someone's sent us ten pounds.'

'It's a hundred you mean!' Sophie shouted, waving it under Martha's nose.

'It never is! I've never seen a cheque for so much in all my life.' Martha said contemplating the cheque again. 'You know what I think? We can put this towards buying a car. We desperately need our own transport.'

'But neither of us can drive?'

'I know, but you're young. You'll soon learn, Captain. I'm too old for such tricks.'

So the decision was taken and when the kind donor heard what they wanted to do with the money, the balance needed to buy a suitable A55 van was added.

Sophie wasn't too sure whether she thought it was such a good idea. The innovation meant she now had to take driving lessons . . . and round and round the back streets she went accompanied by any willing (or unwilling) driver she could find. However, once Lieutenant Barnard had arrived the pressure was off—for she could drive. Whatever Sophie's feelings about learning to drive, she recognised fully the advantages of having their own transport to cut time, energy and expense.

Another occasion brightened the start of 1965. The two officers took part in special meetings at the William Booth Memorial Halls, when tributes were paid to the work of the Goodwill Centre, and £200 was raised for their work. In many ways this was the start of a new phase—for Martha and the Nottingham Goodwill Centre suddenly became news, and she found herself a figure of some public significance. After all, she was one of the Founder's representatives working in the Founder's city in the kind of work dear to his heart in the year celebrating the Founder's greatest achievement.

All of a sudden she was in demand for radio, television and newspaper features on The Salvation Army in general and the work of the Goodwill in particular. It was a natural choice, as the journalists saw it, to interview one of the Army's officers working in and around Booth's first home in Sneinton, Nottingham.

Most of the features were published or broadcast in June when the centenary celebrations took place. Independent Television's 'This Week' programme paid tribute to the Army then, and for part of the programme, Martha's work was filmed, inside the Storer Street Centre (serving lunches to the old people) and in the local park (leading the recently started open-air Sunday school). She visited various of her people living in some of the grim Victorian slum-dwellings around the Centre—most notably Patsy and Stewart and their mother (though of course, no names were mentioned). BBC Television chose to film interviews with the General and other officers, including Martha, for their 'Meeting Point' programme.

Among press tributes several big provincial newspapers carried a series of articles telling the story of The Salvation Army, and two at least, paid visits to the Nottingham Goodwill Centre. Leslie Thomas concluded his series for the *Liverpool Echo*, for instance, with references such as: 'In Nottingham today Booth's battle is neither over nor nearly over. "Sometimes," says Major Martha Field, "I walk these streets and my feet are aching and my heart, too, for that matter, and I look to the sky and say Oh boy, what you've let me in for General!"

'Talk to this round-faced woman, eyes brightly framed in her spectacles, and you get some idea of what such people mean to The Salvation Army, what the Army means to them, and what their combination means to mankind.'

Not to be outdone, Nottingham's own *Evening Post and News* for June 29th, 1965 gave major coverage to Brigadier Martha Field (promoted in May) and spelt out just how full the weekly routine was at the Goodwill: 'Sunday is a hectic day for Brigadier Field,' wrote Jean Davey, the woman's page writer, 'as she leads services, preaches, plays her concertina and sings at about half a dozen meetings, most of them for children in the Centre and in St. Edward's Park nearby. Monday evening brings playtime for the children and a men's club at which the men have a meal. Tuesday night, timbrel practice time for the girls who play at the services. There's an adult service later. Wednesday afternoon there's a mothers' meeting and in the evening a boys' club. Thursday evenings Brigadier Field and her colleagues relax by going to the Divisional Holiness Meeting at the William Booth Memorial Halls and Friday nights she's off with her concertina to sing to the bedridden and to sell The Salvation Army papers in the pubs. "This is a wonderful means of making contact with people," says the Brigadier. Saturday morning the Brigadier visits the sick. And Saturday afternoon is her own.'

In all these articles Martha tried to deflect the reporter's attention away from herself on to incidents, people's needs, funny anecdotes. Though whether Leslie Thomas's quote 'I know how to rifle a gas meter expertly, how to give a woman of ninety a permanent wave, how to get a girl off the streets and how to play the concertina' was quite what Martha expected him to print — is another matter!

Of course, all this unsought publicity had fantastic results. Without doubt nationwide TV and press coverage helped to launch The Salvation Army's special centenary appeal with its slogan 'For God's Sake — Care' on a high tide of public goodwill. It also meant that during 1965, on top of all her other work, Martha for one, became more and more in demand as a speaker, interviewee and as a subject for articles.

Not that she was a stranger to public platforms; and certainly was a most welcome speaker at local rotary club luncheons. Now invitations really began to flood in from all over the place. Martha, refusing to allow the goodwill work to be affected, squeezed in as many meetings as she dared into what little spare time she could afford. They were busy enough without extra engagements as well. At one point that spring, they had been on the go for so long without a proper night's sleep that she and Sophie decided to take the telephone off its hook, a thing they had never done before. Martha went to bed, dropping immediately into a heavy sleep and woke up, with a terrible start, to hear a buzzing noise in her ear. It was the telephone operator trying to get their attention. As soon as Martha picked up the telephone the operator said, 'What happened to you? I've been trying to get you all evening. There's a call for you from the police.'

'Oh dear!' Martha said. 'We were exhausted. We haven't had any sleep for nights . . . We took the telephone off its hook . . .'

'Well, look duck. Don't do it again without telling us. We'll hold the calls for you . . .'

'Oh no. I couldn't bear to do it again . . . What's the trouble?'

The operator put Martha through to the local police and the constable explained that they had a woman from Wolverhampton who had been found soliciting, and who needed a bed for the night. Could they take her? Martha agreed, glancing at the bedside clock. It was one a.m.

In July came Nottingham's own celebrations. Special centenary services were held at the Albert Hall and the Memorial Halls and another turning point for the goodwill arrived. One man converted during the service was to become a good friend of the goodwill team. Brian Hart, a young Nottingham born and bred business man was lent, not long after his conversion, a copy of *God in the Slums* by Hugh Redwood. Deeply moved by what he read, he asked one of the officers at the Corps if such work still existed.

'Come and meet one of our own Slum Sisters,' the officer said and introduced Brian Hart to Captain Sophie Wilson at the back of the Hall. When Sophie heard of his interest she invited him to meet her C.O. and visit the Goodwill Centre for himself.

The house, Brian thought, had seen better days but its interior was a shining example of cleanliness in an area of almost indescribable squalor. He immediately warmed to the quietly spoken Irish officer with her shining eyes and calm face — and her two assistants — one Scots, one English. Martha, for her part, gladly let him see what her work entailed and over the weeks she showed him a side of Nottingham he had never seen before. As Brian's eyes were opened a resolve to do something practical to help took hold of him. He prayed and thought about it, recognising that money was one obvious way. But another pair of hands would prove even more invaluable. In November 1965, when he became a Salvationist, he offered himself to Martha as a full-time unpaid helper.

It is doubtful whether he knew quite what he was taking on. He had received a few hints. For one thing, he and his wife and two daughters went to camp that year to help Martha at Willoughby on the Wolds. For once, Sophie did not have to struggle on her own with the guy ropes of the big boys' tent. And Martha found Mrs. Hart's apparently limitless supply of cotton dresses for the little girls a wonderful help.

Trusting God to provide for her daily needs was a basic way of life for Martha. Praying with her was a revelation for her simple faith produced some amazing results. On one occasion they were about to leave the Goodwill Centre for the usual round of visits, when the telephone rang. It was the almoner from one of the hospitals trying to make certain that an old man being discharged that day from the T.B. sanatorium had a bed for the flat she had found for him. Could the Army help her? Martha promised to do all she could, but on checking with the local Army sources a bed was not available.

'Before we go out we must bring this need before the Lord,' Martha said to Brian and the others. The prayer ended and the front door open, the telephone rang again. This time it was a man who had been clearing out the home of an old aunt. Whilst most of the furniture was useless, there was a very good single bed, with an almost new mattress. Was it of any use to The Salvation Army? Within an hour, Captain Wilson had collected the bed and delivered it to the flat, waiting to make sure all was well when the old man arrived home.

If Brian was under any illusions about his home town when he joined the goodwill team, it did not take long to shatter some of them. On one of his first 'official' visits Martha told him to come in his uniform. He did so, assuming that it was a witness to those they were about to visit. It was to be that—and more. Forest Fields the district they were to visit—had a pleasant sounding name but it had become one of the twilight areas which, as Brian discovered, housed the worst vice centre of the city. In bygone days it had been a select residential area on the edge of the city, but now the urban sprawl of modern buildings had left it to decay. Immigrants, prostitutes, dishonest landlords and the flotsam and jetsam of society were to be found there.

When they first entered the house which was their destination, the stench nearly made Brian sick. But Brigadier Field apparently unaffected, was away up the stairs. Picking his way carefully in the dark Brian followed her till they reached the top floor. A timid, almost frightened voice answered Martha's knock and as soon as she announced herself, the door was opened. A pathetic sight met their eyes. The attic room was not more than 14 feet by 10 feet with one small window, and contained a motley collection of shoddy furniture. It was home for a thin frail 'slip of a girl' as Brian called her, who turned out to be the mother of the other three occupants of the room, three half-caste children aged between a few months old and three years. Brian was struck by the beauty of their big brown eyes, as they gazed at their visitors.

Soon their gaze moved to Martha's hand as it dipped again and again into her 'magic bag'. Nappies, food and sweeties were put on the table and little toys for the three mites. While the toys were being played with, Eve chatted — pouring out her problems as if glad to share them with someone who cared. She had got entangled with a young Pakistani who was the father of the children. He didn't contribute a penny to their upkeep in spite of the fact that there was a court order against him for maintenance. She had no-one to turn to; her mother had been on the streets for years and half-encouraged her daughters to do the same. Her elder sister lived with a West Indian whose 'protection' was the only security she knew. Their father could not care less where his daughters were or how they fared.

Brian was deeply affected by what he saw that day, admitting to Martha later that he went home and wept over the sad fate of those three children and their mother. It had shaken him to see the kind of house that Martha had to enter daily not knowing what reception might await her.

But there was a happier sequel to that visit. They had prayed a great deal about Eve's plight and particularly her longing to leave that attic prison and move away from the sordid life she had been involved in. The rehousing of a family of four seemed well nigh impossible. Then, suddenly, they were offered a small house at Long Eaton, vacant but unfurnished. If they could get it furnished they could move Eve into it almost immediately.

Brian pondered their problem as he started out on the day's routine. If only they could find some furniture . . . If only . . . Perhaps he should take a leaf out of the Brigadier's book and pray about it. He stopped his car and told God that the house was a wonderful answer to prayer but where and how could they find the furniture for it? As he prayed Brian felt a growing certainty that he should go to the big furniture store in the city centre. It seemed like a fool's errand, but he went. When he arrived, it took some courage to go inside and explain his predicament to the manager.

But the man smiled and said, 'Just come through to the back here.' Brian followed him into a huge warehouse, so full of furniture that he could scarcely believe his eyes.

'Help yourself to what you want. This is all secondhand stuff we take in part-exchange . . . we have little or no use for it.'

With the furniture situation sorted out—all the house needed was some carpets. And God met that need the same day also. A lady rang the Centre offering some secondhand carpeting from a relative's home she was clearing . . . would they come and collect it if they wanted it? By that evening, Brian had organised transport for both furniture and carpets out to the house and they had the joy of moving Eve and her children in the next day.

Perhaps of all the places in Martha's 'parish', the conditions in the lodging houses shocked Brian the most. He accompanied Martha on her visits there and found it hard to believe that people could exist in such filth. The landlord who knew the area was to be demolished made no effort to repair or improve broken windows, leaky roofs and rotting floorboards. By this time, too, the police were threatening action against the landlord and the closure of the buildings. This would mean that the men would have nowhere to go. Few of them would go to the Army's men's hostel, because they disliked institutions. Unless alternative accommodation was provided all that was left was derelict buildings and railway arches.

Meanwhile Martha continued her devoted nursing of several of the inmates, accepting fleas, vermin, maggots, smells and vomit, as part of the cost of that particular piece of service. Just occasionally the routine was interrupted by the death of one of her patients — sometimes outside in the street; sometimes inside the lodging houses. On one memorable occasion the man's roommates clubbed together and presented her with a box of chocolates as a sign that they were not so hardened as all that, and fully appreciated what she did when they were ill. Martha was touched by the gift, particularly after it had been made clear that they had bought it and not 'nicked' it.

Probably the incident which brought matters to a head with the local authorities was caused by the man with the knife who attacked Martha. Not only had he attacked her, he had also done damage to other property and tried to harm a young girl. He was sent to prison for six months and the police kept a watchful eye on the houses after that, hoping to close them down.

Martha was a staunch supporter of any move by the council that would benefit her people. It was well known that the slums of St. Ann's were to be demolished . . . it was only a question of time. In the meantime, the Nottingham welfare department were learning just how much Brigadier Field was prepared to co-operate with them if it improved the lot of her people. On one of his many visits to the welfare department, the Salvation Army public relations officer was asked, 'You're not going to take Brigadier Field away from us, are you? We couldn't manage without her.'

The Salvation Army prison officer, Brigadier Head, also continued to ask for her assistance. One prisoner wanted his family visited and the children invited to the Goodwill

Centre for he hoped they would eventually be dedicated there. Martha agreed to call, and accepted the offer of a lift from a friend. They drove a fair distance in bitterly cold weather, only to find the prisoner's five children ill with measles. They were not in bed but lying on chairs downstairs, covered in coats. There was no coal and no decent bedclothes to keep them warm. After she had shared the goodies she had brought with them, she drove quickly back to the quarters so that she could ring the coal merchants. Then, with the help of the Children's Officer, blankets, food and bedding were supplied and they returned with these.

Once the children were fully recovered they duly attended the Sunday school and their mother came too. A warm relationship developed with the family and soon there was the thrill of their father's release from prison. The promise was kept and the children dedicated, with Brigadier Head conducting the service. The hall at Storer Street was packed for the occasion, the family's Welfare Officer attending. The family continued to come to the Army regularly and it was a particular joy for Martha to see their daughter Rose enrolled as a junior soldier, and the father helping at the Centre.

Another moment of joy was to see the wonder on the face of a homeless little boy, one Bank Holiday weekend, when he received new clothes and saw God at work. He was the eldest of a family of homeless children brought to the Centre. His clothes were in such a state they had either to be soaked or cut off his body. Pyjamas could be found but no boy's clothes . . . and all the shops were shut. As she put him to bed, Martha said, 'Well, Derek, only the Lord knows where we are going to find clothes for you so let's say our prayers and ask Him.'

The next morning, quite early, a knock at the door revealed a woman with a case full of boy's clothes — shoes, socks, everything. They fitted Derek so well he was thrilled, saying, 'Eh, this suit and shoes are smashing. God must have known you were looking for them!'

The children's reactions to things usually delighted her, but just now and then they would catch her out!

'Who killed Goliath?' asked Martha of the Sunday school at Storer Street.

'William Booth,' came the smart reply from one lad, who added in his defence, when corrected, 'Well, you're always telling us about him and how wonderful he was.'

Then there were the occasions when she expected naughtiness and had a pleasant surprise. Richard and Terry were brothers who had first come to the Goodwill Centre after watching and joining in the Open-air Sunday school in the summer of 1965. Poorly dressed but very keen, they were soon among the regulars at Storer Street, always in their places on time and singing the choruses lustily. Decision Sunday arrived, and a special invitation was given for any child who wished to invite Jesus into their lives to come forward.

The hall was packed, yet not a sound could be heard. Then a tell-tale shuffling began among the boys, so often the prelude to a prank of some kind. Leaving Sophie to continue the service at the front Martha walked down the aisle to see what was happening. The noise was coming from the back row where Richard and Terry were sitting. Gradually she discovered that Richard wanted to go forward — but had a big hole in his shoes. He was trying on the shoes of a friend, but they did not fit so various whispered snippets of advice were being shared with him. 'Eh Richard. You kneel in the one's you 'as on,' Martha overheard one lad say. 'God doesna look at yer shoes. 'E looks at yer 'eart.'

After a bit more shuffling, Richard decided this was sensible talk and he went forward as silence fell once more.

Martha followed him to the front, willing the children not to giggle at the hole in his shoes. No-one did.

Another friend they made through the Open-air Sunday school was slightly older. Harry the Roadsweeper was in his forties, in fact, and had been attracted by the sight of the children singing their action choruses to Martha's concertina in the park on Sundays. Naturally Martha had noticed his interest and invited him in to the Sunday evening service and the weeknight meetings. With his friend Jack, Harry became a regular, and eventually, kneeling at the Mercy Seat, asked God to come into his heart and life.

It was not to be his only appearance there. For a man just a little too fond of his drink, Harry found it hard to say goodbye to the bottle. For weeks he would resist the temptation, then have another period on the drink, asking God's forgiveness again when he made a further effort to mend his ways.

On one of these occasions Captain Wilson knelt with him, helping him to understand that God did not condemn him for his weakness and loved him still. Later in conversation with Martha Sophie said, 'You know something? Somehow tonight with Harry it was different. He asked God to prepare him to meet his mother in heaven, and he's never done that before as far as I know.'

That Sunday was Harry's last at the Goodwill Centre. He was run over while working on his job and died during that week. His prayer to meet his mother was answered.

Martha's joys might be varied, but then so were her disappointments. One of the most difficult tasks she tackled in Nottingham was trying to befriend the local 'totties' (as prostitutes are called in the local jargon) or to dissuade a girl from going on with such a way of life. Many girls made promises — but few kept them. Some actually gave up the 'game' only to go back to it later. Martha was not sure which was worse.

Brian Hart accompanied her on several forays into the twilight housing areas, where many of these girls were accommodated, often living with the men who were living off their earnings. A man's presence was always useful on such occasions. Eve represented just one of those whom Martha asked him to help her with.

One Sunday morning she went with Brian, by arrangement, to collect a girl living with a coloured man in a notorious house in the neighbourhood. When they climbed the stairs and knocked at the door, someone called, 'Who's there?'

'The Salvation Army,' Martha called back.

There was silence. The door remained closed ... behind them another opened on the landing above. A woman of about thirty-five years of age peered down asking weakly, 'Can you help me?' Martha climbed the stairs immediately, noticing, as the woman led her into the room, that there was blood on her head. Sitting her down quickly on the bed, Martha investigated the cut under the implacable eyes of two coloured men.

'What happened?' Martha asked.

'I got this on the streets last night,' the girl said indicating the cut. 'And he's taken my money from me!' she added vehemently, pointing at one of the men.

'Why not come back with me so that I can treat that cut properly?' Martha bravely suggested. 'You are welcome to stay with us until it heals . . .'

The woman would not be persuaded, deterred by the silent presence of the men. Sadly Martha had to treat the cut and leave her there, and she and Brian felt it had been a wasted journey.

The next day Martha was due to travel to the annual Officers' Conference in Derbyshire. As she was packing she glanced out of the window to see a young woman standing outside the Centre. At her feet was a holdall and her pale upturned face was familiar. It was the woman from the house they had visited the day before.

'I've come,' she said, simply when Martha ran down to open the door.

'I am glad,' Martha replied, already making plans so that the girl could stay with friends while they were away.

Another ex-prostitute, Ruth, began attending the Army meetings and sought God's help to change her ways. Martha had knelt with her, and spent many hours in the weeks that followed, encouraging her to start a new way of life in God's strength. It was a bitter blow after four months of progress to receive the news that Ruth had been seen soliciting again. Martha attended the Thursday night Holiness meeting that week, low in spirit and wondering just where things had gone wrong. It made her want to weep. As she fought with her feeling of failure and disappointment, the sweet voice of the soloist for the evening penetrated her gloom. The words she was singing seemed to Martha a reminder that she must not let her feelings drag her down, she must press on forgetting the past. She listened as the refrain came again: 'I am praying, blessed Master, to be more and more like Thee.' A new sense of courage helped to restore her spirits.

How hard it was to see innocent children caught up in the sordid lives of their parents. One young lad whose mother was on the streets keeping the father, said to Martha one day 'I wish Jesus lived in my house.'

Martha put her arms round him, lost for words. Usually she could point to the love of parents for each other and for their children. But she knew how little that love was evident in his home.

'Well, Tom, Jesus lives in people,' she said choosing her words carefully, 'Good people, like doctors and nurses and people who serve others and love others. They can come to your home. And you can take Jesus home in your heart too.'

'An' you're not making a bad job of it either, are you?' he put in, much to Martha's surprise.

15

The Pace Quickens

If 1965 had seemed busy, 1966 proved no easier. The pace was certainly showing no signs of slackening. Martha was still in great demand as a speaker, while inquiries, gifts and visitors continued to arrive at Storer Street in a steady flow.

Hugh Redwood arrived unexpectedly that year. Sophie and Martha had been caring for a retired Salvation Army Major who was bedridden and seriously ill. One day, as Martha was attending to the officer's needs, she heard foot-steps on the stairs, which she assumed to be the doctor's. Turning round she was amazed to see the equally surprised but beaming Hugh Redwood, bouquet of flowers in hand.

'Well, what a surprise!' they exclaimed, almost in unison, and soon she and her patient were listening to his explanation. It had been only on an impulse that the retired Fleet Street journalist had decided to visit Nottingham to see the retired Major, not knowing that his old friend Martha Field was working in the city.

When his visit to the officer was completed Martha asked him if he would join her and Sophie for lunch. He said he would love to as long as it wasn't putting her to any trouble.

'No, in fact you'll be doing us a favour,' Martha ex-plained as they walked back to Storer Street. 'You see, last night, we cooked this chicken for someone who didn't arrive. We were so put out — because we don't buy chicken for ourselves, it's too expensive — we couldn't bring ourselves to eat it. So it's there, untouched.'

Hugh Redwood laughed. 'There, the Lord must have known I was going to come today, and He's even provided a chicken for me!'

Gladys Aylward, and her adopted son, Gordon, came to the Goodwill Centre that year also; another 'small woman' with a big heart. Martha had a warm regard for her, having heard her speak at officers' conferences. And Miss Aylward helped to make her feel like a queen — for when Martha confessed that the week's housekeeping was spent and she was 'broke', Gladys Aylward turned and looked out of the front window of Storer Street, to the crowded rows of narrow alleyways and terraced dwellings.

'My dear girl,' she said. 'Never say you're broke. Look what you've got. All those people out there. And I've got all the people of Formosa.'

With their busy routine continuing, there were three major developments in the Goodwill work during 1966 — for the old, the young and for the men in the lodging houses.

The first innovation was a happy result of Martha's contact with the Rotary Clubs of Nottingham and its surrounding districts. The members of one such club offered to pay for a week's seaside holiday at Butlins, Skegness, for fifty older people who would otherwise not have a holiday. They also made sure that coaches were booked to take the holidaymakers there and back, but they asked Martha to arrange for the right people to be invited and then prepared for the trip.

It was quite a palaver! Packing for and picking up the folk from numerous addresses and getting them to the coaches in time for the grand civic send-off in front of the Council House with the Lord Mayor of Nottingham doing the honours . . . was pretty exhausting, and only possible with the help of many volunteers. Many of the old people had never been away since their childhood and the two coachloads of happy suntanned veterans who returned a week later, had only one complaint — they'd been given too much to eat!

The second major development that year benefited the children and arose out of the plight of many of Martha's poorer youngsters who depended for their regular nourishment on their school dinners. Come the long summer holidays and even that source of food would disappear. ' 'Ere's a tanner ter get yerself some chips.' This was what the lucky ones were told, by parents who were working all day.

After negotiations with the officers at the William Booth Memorial Halls it was agreed that the Goodwill Officers could use the hall to serve hot lunches twice a week. Sixty children was the maximum they could manage, listed for them by the local school authorities as qualifying for free school meals. Not content with feeding their bodies, the officers decided to provide games and activities to help keep them off the streets.

As a result, every Tuesday and Thursday, throughout the school holidays, the hall opened in the mornings for games and singing activities led by helpers, while the meal was prepared and served. The money to pay for the food was raised by the Salvation Army officers, BBC local radio helped bring in a donation towards the cost, and meat and vegetables were given by local traders. The welfare department was in full support of the move, grateful to the Army for shouldering yet another need.

The popularity of the 'free' dinners was immense and special 'meal tickets' had to be issued to prevent gatecrashers. The corps officer on the door one day, asked a little boy accompanied by his brother, why he'd only got one ticket.

' 'E ain't got one, mister, 'cos 'e's come in another boy's place, who can't come today.'

'Oh I see. What's this other boy's name, so I can tick it then?'

'Er – I dunno what 'is name is,' the boy replied. 'But that's 'im sitting over there. You can ask 'im yerself!'

That autumn, Martha included the story in her address at the Nottingham Rotary Clubs' Civic Day, in front of the Lord Mayor, the Sheriff of Nottingham and the Town Clerk. She was more nervous than she had ever been for it was an important occasion. But, as always, just talking very simply about 'her people' and using that story really helped to break the ice. When she saw their faces breaking into smiles and heard their laughter, she could relax and move quickly to the more serious matters, holding their attention in a different way.

She spoke also to the Bulwell and Basford Inner Wheel Club's Anniversary. Knowing many of them were mothers, she told them about some of her children and the young mothers she knew, explaining that, as The Salvation Army had no maternity home in Nottingham, the Goodwill Centre kept a room specially for the use of needy girls.

Her talks must have gone home, because some of her hearers acted upon them, and asked if they could assist her in any way. Raising money was an obvious help, but she was always pleased to have offers of practical assistance. When one group asked if they could help serve Christmas lunches to the housebound Martha gladly agreed. She accepted help to cook thirty Christmas dinners for the volunteers to take round in their cars, then a further sixty to serve to the people who came to the Centre on foot, or were brought by friends.

The third big development during 1966 was a glad yet

sad change: the closure of the lodging houses. The man who owned the two in Storer Street was taken ill and rushed to hospital. The local authorities, hearing that he was not 'in residence', slapped an order on the houses, as unfit for habitation and closed them. The occupants were put out in the street, the places cleared of their miserable contents which were taken away to the city incinerator, and the rooms were fumigated and sealed up.

Martha was relieved to see the last of those terrible gaunt rooms, but appalled that seventy men could be just left to roam the streets with nowhere to go. In a desperate effort to help she asked the Corps officer at the Memorial Halls and Brian Hart, to organise a 'soup run' that night to see if any of the men could be found and helped. She supplied the hot soup and fresh rolls, and the men the transport. But after searching derelict buildings, demolition sites, and various other haunts, only one or two men were found. None would accept the offer of a bed in the Army's men's hostel. It seemed, to Brian in particular, a very unsatisfactory end to the business. The action of the authorities appeared callous, and most of the men in the houses already felt they had been illtreated by society. This would only increase that feeling.

The closing of the lodging houses changed the face of Storer Street irrevocably, though not for long. Soon, the demolition gangs with their bulldozers were going to move in and the scandal of the slums of St. Ann's was to be eradicated for ever.

The compulsory rehousing of tenants meant many of their friends and neighbours would soon be in new accommodation for the first time in their lives. For the Goodwill Centre it was not so straightforward, and once again, Martha was looking for suitable premises, knowing that the question of compensation would be sorted out when the moment arose. The 'good years' at Storer Street were coming to an end. It was also, though she probably did not fully realise it, the start of a completely new chapter in the Goodwill work of the Army.

She was aware that new needs were emerging — that there had been a growing need in Nottingham to give shelter to homeless women and girls; that the lack of a local Army women's hostel meant that the Centre had had to help where it could, taking in girls on the run, girls on probation, as well as girls and mothers with nowhere to go. Homelessness in Britain was fast emerging as the scourge of the 'never had it so good' sixties with Shelter and 'Cathy Come Home' acting as conscience prickers to a nation a little too complacent with itself. Pressure groups and public opinion forced local authorities to look into their housing schemes and make provision for the homeless.

Brian Hart, knowing the plight of the Goodwill Officers, had been keeping his eyes and ears open for possibilities. He arrived at Storer Street one day, with news of a property he had found which seemed to have a lot to offer. It was a good deal bigger but this could be an advantage, and Martha and Sophie were taken to view it. It turned out to be a vacant Church Army hostel in Peel Street, a fair distance from Storer Street to the west. The tall double-fronted detached building set high above the sloping street, seemed huge. It had a wide side entrance where they could park their van, and outbuildings at the rear. Inside it was spotlessly clean and very big. Martha was used to having just a moderately sized house to look after, accommodating her and her assistants and one or two visitors. Here she could sleep thirty, with the largest bedroom taking twelve beds, the others less.

Downstairs there was a large lounge for 'guests' and to the right of the front door a big dining-room, with a hatch for serving meals, cooked in the roomy square kitchen at the back. At the rear of the house was a long high room that she could envisage using as their hall for meetings. It lacked something of the homeliness and intimacy of the Storer Street hall, but would look a lot better when they had installed the platform at one end.

Yes, the place certainly had possibilities. Eventually it was agreed in early 1967 that negotiations to rent the house should be made, though it would take some time to prepare it for its new function. In the meantime, Martha was only too glad to make use of its lovely kitchen for a major cooking spree whenever the need arose. Various activities began to emanate from Peel Street during the months that preceded its official opening in late 1967.

Many kind friends, organisations and groups, responded to the appeal for help in equipping the larger premises with fittings and furniture, and in spite of a bad attack by vandals on the empty property which stripped it of lead and other vital fittings worth £300, the place was ready when opening day dawned.

Not that the whole year had been spent in house-hunting and moving. Martha as usual had far too much else to do, continuing the work at Storer Street. But by the summer the Peel Street kitchen began to prove its worth, cooking a batch of sixty hot dinners twice a week for the children on holiday from school.

Then the Rotary Clubs of Bulwell and Basford asked if Martha would repeat her performance of 1966, by taking a party away on a Butlin's holiday again. This time it was to be 100 needy children and she was not only responsible for selecting the lucky ones, but also helping to prepare them for their holiday.

Martha found it hard to resist the foibles of some of her children in their efforts to win her approval . . . and a place at camp. 'Decision Sunday' inevitably brought its crop of sudden 'conversions'. She and Sophie had guessed something of the sort would happen, and, sure enough, one of their naughtiest boys, Billy, was out kneeling at the front. Sophie looked hard at Martha with her 'I told you so' expression and Martha, hiding a smile, went to talk with the boy. She asked if she could help him.

'I'm tellin' the Lord I wanna go ter camp. An' I'm tellin' yer, if yer let's me go — I'll be a good boy and be a real help.'

Martha looked very seriously at him. 'Now Billy, I'm sorry to have to say this. But you see, you promised me exactly the same thing two years running. And there's been no sign of you trying to change your ways . . . I'm afraid you can't go to camp.'

Martha thought that was the end of it. But when the kind gentleman from the Rotarians called for Billy's sister, to take her to camp, he found Billy ready with his case packed as well.

'I'm going along as a helper for Brigadier,' Billy explained, and not knowing the circumstances of the case, he was driven to Skegness. There, on his arrival, the man discovered Billy wasn't booked in.

'He said he was to come as a helper so I brought him,' he told Martha, while Billy tried to look nonchalant. Martha accepted the situation gracefully and allowed him to stay — as long as he really helped. And he did.

Martha was able to spend only the first four days with the children at camp, but it was long enough to make sure every child had the right clothing and the right amount of spending money, divided up to spread out over the whole week. Brian Hart was left in charge in her absence and had some vivid memories to recount to her on his return.

There had been the nightly comedy sequence which occurred when they were putting the over-active youngsters to bed. One pair of children would be tucked in, their chalet door closed, and the helper would go to the adjoining chalet to settle down the next pair. By the time the second couple had been tucked in the first pair would be up again and running around the outside of their chalet. And by the time they had been caught and put back to bed the second pair would be up and doing the same thing — and so it went on until exhaustion set in!

Mealtimes were another revelation. As Brian reported to Martha, one boy, asked if he would like hot or cold milk on his cornflakes said, 'Milk? We just 'as 'ot water at 'ome!' Another anxiously watched his cereal plate disappear to be replaced by a plate of egg and bacon and exclaimed 'Cor! You gets two breakfasses 'ere.' And yet another, spreading an ample portion of butter on his toast, commented, 'Hey, the margarine they gives you don't arf taste different.'

Another pleasant development during 1967 resulted from the publicity given to the needs of the Goodwill work in Nottingham during the Diamond Jubilee year of the Army's Home League's Helping Hand scheme. The raising of funds to provide a proper 'Emergency Mobile Unit' for Nottingham was suggested as a suitable anniversary present and its arrival that year was not before time. The secondhand A55 van, bought in 1965, had given up the ghost after much stalwart service, and it had never been ideal for the larger demands of their work. The new van was purpose-built and much better equipped, with lockers for blankets and First Aid, and urns for serving hot drinks to injured or workers with the emergency services, if a disaster occurred. If the sirens sounded in the city and news of a big fire reached Martha's ears, the van was soon stocked up with hot fluids and on its way.

Moving to Peel Street meant taking the Goodwill work into a new area away from Sneinton, and this was a challenge in every way. She had to keep in touch with her 'regulars' from Storer Street until the demolition work began. But she now had a completely new 'parish' to visit. With a special team of officers drawn from the local corps, she and Sophie organised the visitation and made new friends.

Among these, were an elderly couple in their late eighties who were having a dreadful struggle to cope. Mrs. Evans was unable to use the stairs and Mr. Evans had to carry his wife up and down each day . . . until he tripped and fell with his precious burden. Then Martha was called in. Fortunately he was near the bottom of the stairs and did not fall far — but the shock set the old lady back. Martha nursed her through the final stages of her illness then took on the daily burden of nursing Mr. Evans, popping in to care for him at home, until he also died — two years later.

One of the regulars she was still visiting near Storer Street involved more dedication than she could have imagined. Mrs. Simmons had been a prostitute but had come to realise that she needed God. This was after Martha, who met her out shopping, had invited her to attend the meetings. She began to come regularly and much prayer was made for her. It was an overjoyed Martha who knelt beside her at the Penitent Form one Sunday evening, listening to her prayer for forgiveness and a new life.

It was a further joy to see her face radiate a new peace and happiness. She never missed a meeting after that, enjoying her new faith and new friends.

But all was not well. She began to lose weight suddenly and look worn and ill. A visit to the doctor, then the specialist, confirmed that she had cancer of the stomach. She must have treatment. She refused to go into hospital, preferring to be in her own home. Her bed was moved downstairs and kind neighbours and the Salvation Army officers helped to care for her.

Over the ensuing weeks, visiting her became more and more trying because of the smell. Even in the cold weather, they had to keep the door on to the street open to allow some fresh air and relief to the woman struggling for breath. Mrs. Simmons suffered greatly and the end came slowly.

One lunchtime a neighbour called Martha away from serving the meal at the centre because Mrs. Simmons was dying. Collecting her bag and overall, Martha hurried through the streets to find the woman barely conscious. When Martha took her hand, her eyelids fluttered and opened and she tried to smile. Weakly she said, 'The Lord is my shepherd,' adding a little later, 'Thank you for finding me.' At last, her suffering was over.

Alone, Martha had to cope with the last services to the body, not a pleasant task in the circumstances. Buoyed on by her thankfulness for Mrs. Simmons' final testimony, and with a surgical mask liberally soaked in disinfectant, she somehow found the strength to complete all that was necessary.

16

Yes! – For God Called Me

The 'new' Goodwill Centre at Peel Street was officially opened on November 16th, 1967, by the Lord Mayor and Lady Mayoress of Nottingham with the Army's British Commissioner William Cooper assisting. The big hall at the rear of the building was packed. For the benefit of the visitors the official programme explained 'From the Goodwill Centre, a regular round-the-clock ministry is directed to those in need. In addition, a rest room and meal centre is open to the elderly, bathing facilities for the aged are provided. An emergency care unit is also in operation for those who would be directed by the Welfare Authorities. For the community, there is also the evangelical side of the work being carried on at women's meetings, Sunday school and clubs for the children.'

No mention was made of the future use of the building as a hostel for the homeless, though it cannot have been many weeks later before Martha found herself looking after families and not just one or two girls brought by the police.

Originally Martha had thought that the 'annexe' Brian Hart had shown her, would be used to house 'a few' people. But by 1968 the few began to be many and gradually the numbers built up to over thirty.

The turning point was the request by Nottingham

Council to use Peel Street as their official 'hostel for the homeless'. The city lacked such a welfare unit, and The Salvation Army felt this was a chance to pioneer a new work and serve the city as well — with grants from the City Council for the upkeep of the service.

Martha and Sophie were at the hub of this 'experiment' and suddenly found themselves swamped. At any time of night or day, there would be requests for accommodation for families — women and children at first; then after 'Cathy Come Home' — fathers as well. Lacking sufficient staff, the two officers were worked off their feet trying to run two things at once — a goodwill centre serving the local community, as at Storer Street, and a social and welfare unit serving the homeless of the city. On top of all this, Martha was still being invited to speak about the work at schools, police cadet courses, townswomen's guilds, women's institutes and many other places, including her old 'training college'.

Martha's heart, if the truth be known, was still in the Goodwill work — out visiting the needy people in their homes, knocking on doors and meeting new people, not waiting for need to come knocking on their door at Peel Street, as it so often did, in the shape of needy families.' Of course, she served them as she had served people all her life, but the strain of the change in routine was beginning to tell.

Many cases touched her deeply. A little boy of six, deserted by his mother, was brought in by his father who was to spend the night in the Men's Hostel. When she took off the boy's shoes, his feet were sore and blistered because they had been forced into shoes that were too small. She tucked him up in the pretty room they had allocated for children, near their quarters. Having helped him say his prayers she asked if there was anything else he wanted. With all the gravity he could muster he told her that though he was only six, he had spent seven years in Australia, then added, 'My mum left me before I could walk. Please can I have a goodnight kiss?' As she hugged and kissed him the tears stood in Martha's eyes, for he should have known his own mother's love.

All things considered, new and unknown terrors lurked in their new work at Peel Street. Offering accommodation to a number of strangers meant that problem people, and occasionally dangerous ones, were living on the premises — something that Martha had not had to face before.

They learnt lessons the hard way — particularly about drug addicts. Not long after they had moved in Martha admitted a young girl, who was brought to her as being 'in need of care and attention', having been found sleeping rough. No-one appeared to have discovered that the girl was also a drug addict in need of special treatment. She was in fact desperate for drugs — or money to obtain them . . .

Sophie was busy laying lino upstairs when her colleague was attacked by the girl. Unaware of the drama below, she continued happily banging away with the hammer and tacks, not hearing Martha's desperate cries for help. The girl had butted her in the stomach and winded her so badly that her calls were not loud at first. Then as she got her breath back, her arms were nearly twisted out of their sockets as the girl continued to pummel her.

'Captain! Captain!' she shouted again, thankful at last to hear 'Coming!' and then Sophie's footsteps on the stairs. Sophie's startled expression soon changed to one of concern as she saw Martha's plight. A firm hand forced the girl to release Martha's wrists, and together the officers tried to calm her down while the police were called.

The mentally sick were also difficult residents, though not usually through any fault of their own. Martha took in one mother and her three children found sleeping in a shelter. It was obvious, soon after, that the woman was suffering from a severe mental breakdown. It was a traumatic time, as the woman's disturbed behaviour affected the other residents, particularly at night. Martha, to prevent distress to others, moved the woman's bed into her own room. In the night she was wakened by a scratching noise. The woman was on the floor tearing at the boards with her bare hands. From what Martha could gather, she believed her husband had murdered her baby and buried its body there. Though it was hard to have to do it, Martha and Sophie decided the mother should enter hospital for treatment while the three little ones remained with them, for the time being.

As before Martha and Sophie were still called out to visit people in need. One late telephone call to Peel Street came from a young girl in a call box. She was distressed and incoherent.

'Oh, can you help me please ... We've run this party — a drugs party — and I'm a polio victim and I'm in a terrible way. The drug seems to have done something queer to my limbs and they've all swollen, I don't know what to do ...'

Sophie managed to find out which call box it was and quickly got the mobile unit out and drove there as fast as she could. When she arrived the girl was in such a bad state that it was obviously hospital, and not the hostel, that was the right place for her. Furthermore, there had been others at the party equally badly affected — it sounded like a police matter.

The constable who arrived to check the story agreed that the girl had better go straight to hospital, where she was admitted immediately. She remained there for three weeks, and both Martha and Sophie were able to visit her. She was truly grateful for their care and interest, having confessed to the doctor that she had rung The Salvation Army instead of one of the hospital casualty departments because 'I knew they'd care!'

The co-operation of the police and the welfare department could usually be relied upon — but then they in their turn, depended on the willingness of the Goodwill Officers to help with some of the city's pressing social problems. At any time the telephone at Peel Street would ring and it would be yet another request for help from a social worker, children's officer, probation or police officer. One night, Martha was called out of bed twice to admit three young girls and a baby of seven months.

In the terrible cold of that winter, there was a spate of horrific fires in the crowded housing conditions, where immigrant families were using unsafe paraffin stoves. There was a string of requests for help to accommodate families made homeless by fire. Martha and Sophie tried their best to comfort and calm the shocked and distressed parents, some of whom had tragically lost children in the blaze. Consoling heartbroken people was not made easier by language problems — but a sympathetic arm around the shoulders, a smile and a hot drink could work wonders.

One family they were asked to accommodate at short notice had not lost a child — but were about to gain one. Martha was so worried that she arranged for the couple to have the room next to the quarters, and asked the doctor to call. Lending the mother a nightie for the medical examination, she was startled to find, when she showed the doctor into the room, that mum was in bed, fully dressed with her turban on her head and the nightie on top of her clothes!

The doctor seemed to take it all in his stride, however, having dealt with this kind of situation many times before. He explained to Martha later that the woman thought if she took her clothes off they would be stolen. Any suspicions about the two officers must have been allayed during their stay, for some months afterwards, the whole family came in their Sunday best to say thank you, and to present the officers with a bunch of flowers.

Perhaps more than ever before, the larger demands of Peel Street meant that Martha depended on the help and support of their many 'friends' to keep them in business. It had been true before the new Centre opened, and in her 'vote of thanks' at the thanksgiving service, Martha already had a lengthy list of benefactors to mention. In the months that followed her thanks were expressed again on platforms, in letters and personally.

Martha's experience of timely answers to prayer continued also. Even though her circumstances had changed, God's faithfulness continued to strengthen her. During the crisis time of the fires, she had been asked to supply blankets for a homeless family and had been short of one very necessary one. Standing by the linen cupboard, Martha was telling the Lord about it when the doorbell rang. It was an old friend, a corps officer from Stapleford.

'I've brought you this blanket, Brigadier,' she said, offering Martha a large parcel. 'I thought you might find it useful.' Martha stood, speechless, her eyes fixed in amazement on her fellow officer.

As the unabated flow of homeless families continued to fill Peel Street, Martha and Sophie were faced with several dilemmas. If anything — as 1968 passed — the pace gathered momentum. One or two families in care were one thing; thirty or forty people was another. They demanded a lot of time and energy, catering and organisation. And Martha and Sophie, though they had part-time help, did not have enough staff to cope.

They had to be up at all hours, taking in families, and, if one of their local people was taken sick, they would be out nursing them. It was nothing unusual for Martha to have sat up all night with a dying woman, then return to the

Centre to cook the breakfast for the thirty residents and do a full day's duties.

Martha also attempted to carry on fulfilling the numerous speaking engagements about her work. Often these were at luncheon clubs, and a car would call for her and bring her back afterwards, so that she could carry on her routine as if she'd barely been away. It increased interest in the goodwill work, which often brought in gifts and voluntary help. It was also very exhausting.

Disappointment was exhausting at any time. Sometimes the battle to get a girl 'off the game', for instance, drained Martha of all her usual stoicism. Often the forces of evil appeared to have triumphed. She had not given up her forays into the notorious red light district of the city — wisely taking male support.

Her men companions, usually officers from the local corps, wondered at her temerity and tenacity, especially on one occasion, when she was faced with the body of a dead white woman in a room full of coloured men. Certainly, girls on drugs and girls 'on the game' were among her toughest assignments. The former were dangerous, the latter stubborn. Rebuffs were common in her appeals to the prostitutes but she always stuck to her guns. If they wanted help and shelter they could come to Peel Street.

What little time Martha had to spare, over the years, she had used to keep in touch with old friends. Usually it was by letter, and in this way she remained in contact with people from her Belfast corps days, training college and from her various appointments — Bristol, Manchester, Liverpool, Belfast, Greenock. She was not a great letter writer, but she did like to drop a line to people.

During 1968, Martha casually mentioned to Sophie that she was writing to an old friend in Liverpool, a Salvation Army officer, whose wife, a dear friend of hers, had died some years before. Sophie gave little thought to the matter as she knew her colleague kept in touch with many people. But she had good reason to recall the conversation when Martha announced, late in 1968, that she was to marry Lt.-Colonel Wilfrid Osborne in May 1969

Poor Sophie! She was astounded. But the surprise was not hers alone. Martha herself, had always maintained that she had been far too busy all her life to think about marriage. So there were good reasons for surprise among her many friends.

The wedding ceremony in May 1969 at the William Booth Memorial Halls, was a triumphant occasion. Not only were friends and colleagues present, but 'half of Nottingham as well' as one eye-witness put it. Martha's fame was such that the city seemed to have turned out to see 'their Brigadier' married. Young and old, the well-dressed as well as the not-so-well-dressed, mingled in the gathering, happy to share the bridal couple's joy.

If, during the ceremony, tears could be seen on Captain Wilson's cheeks, it was not just because it was a moving occasion and she was a 'big soft lamb', as Martha put it. Sophie was losing a co-worker who was very dear to her. Martha's marriage meant her retirement after thirty-five years from Goodwill work to join her husband in Liverpool. But her love and loyalty for Nottingham folk was so strong that she cut short her honeymoon to return and conduct the funeral of a friend.

Of course, 'retirement' was not quite the right word for Martha Osborne's new role. As always she could not sit still while there was work to be done, and in due course, she and her husband became 'wardens' to a block of flats for elderly people living under a sheltered housing scheme in Liverpool. Martha's particular gifts of caring and service were soon in action and Wilfrid saw to the administration and general upkeep of the house.

But Martha did have a little more time, at last, to reflect

on her years in the Goodwill. She looked back with amazement and joy, remembering the many people she had come to know and love, some of whom she had brought into the Christian faith and into the ranks of the Army.

The weekend of October 7th to 9th, 1972, stood out in Martha's memories of Nottingham for many reasons. Not least because she and Wilfrid were the 'guests of honour' and she was the speaker at special public meetings to celebrate the first anniversary of the Army's new purpose-built Goodwill Complex in Sneinton, based around the Founder's birthplace.

As they were shown round she was amazed at all the changes. First of all the slums had gone. As they drove up the hill it was apparent that North Street had been pulled down — and later she was shown the empty flattened site of Storer Street. But preserved amid the new modern blocks of flats and ranch-style houses stood Number 12 Notintone Place with its two companions in a little Georgian Square dominated by a statue of William Booth who appeared to be gazing over Nottingham's busy city, his hand pointing upwards, showing a better way to all who might take the trouble to look.

To the left of the square and behind Number 12 lay the 'complex' which was both a Goodwill Centre and an Eventide Home for fifty elderly men and women. My! Martha had never expected anything quite as grand. It was all gleaming fittings, easy-to-clean floors, well-equipped kitchens and offices with a spacious hall and recreation rooms. Upstairs she was shown a new development — flats for homeless families. The need was still great, and it was good to discover that Peel Street was continuing its work. She'd heard rumours that the new 'complex' would make Peel Street redundant and had wondered if it was wise. She was still convinced that there were desperate social needs which could be best met at grassroots level in the more well-worn facilities of a place like Storer Street or Peel Street.

As the officers explained to her the purpose of the 'flats' at the complex, she could recognise the value of this 'second-stage' work. Families first taken into care at Peel Street, could move into one of the flats at the complex for a trial period, before being rehoused. With specially trained Salvation Army officers and welfare workers, the families were given every encouragement to learn how to keep a home, plan a budget, look after their children, and generally cope with the responsibility of having a place of their own. Then when a house was found, the Army and the local welfare department would see that the needy family had all the necessities for equipping it — furniture, bedding, kitchen equipment — and the assurance of regular visits to check on any problems.

When Martha read the anniversary brochure, she came across a new name — 'Community Service Centre'. Under this title the complex was doing many of the jobs she and Sophie had handled at Storer Street: luncheon clubs, meals on wheels, and young people's clubs. But a playgroup operating five days a week was new to her, as was the caravan helping to give the deprived youngsters holidays away from Nottingham.

As she sat on the platform of the big light and airy Hall, her mind could not help comparing all the modern facilities with some of the worst and primitive conditions she'd had to face at North Street, and in the 'good years' at Storer Street and the pioneering of Peel Street — all in old, and much-used buildings. 'If I'm honest,' she thought, 'my heart would still be in the kind of Slum work we did at Storer Street. But it's wonderful that at last the city has a permanent Goodwill Centre and a proper memorial to William Booth.'

Then her eyes caught sight of some of the Army's top

ranking officers who had come to join in thanking God for the new 'complex'. It was still something of an amazement to Martha that her leaders had kept her all those years. For she hadn't been good at coping with the paperwork, and her accounts were often sent late to headquarters.

But the Army had been very patient with her — perhaps because they knew she was getting on with the job and disliked red tape. Martha had a strong feeling that the Founder would have been patient too, so long as the real work was being done.

Her eyes strayed to the row of Goodwill Officers from the complex beside her on the platform. The day of the 'Slum Sister' had certainly changed. In charge of the goodwill side of the complex was a married couple with a staff of some twenty men and women. At the training college, men and women cadets learnt to cope with specialist problems that hadn't been thought of when she was in training: working with the handicapped, the deaf and dumb, with alcoholics or drug addicts. New problems had demanded new techniques.

Finally her eyes turned to survey the faces of the gathering. So many dear friends were there — Salvationists, local welfare officers, rotary and inner wheel members, and many who were 'her people'. What good friends the Goodwill work had had. Whatever would she have done and how could this new complex have been possible without them?

Martha — in her usual self-effacing way did not recognise that this project had become a reality because of her dedication . . . It was her willingness to stick it out in North Street and start an entirely new work at Peel Street that had weighed so strongly in the Army's negotiations with the city fathers for the new Centre. The Salvation Army public relations officer who handled the fund-raising for the complex acknowledged that the Nottingham City Corporation had made a substantial grant towards the cost and, though he had negotiated that grant, 'the Corporation were greatly influenced in their decision by the work and life of Brigadier Martha Field.'

So in many ways the new Centre was a memorial not only to William Booth, but to the dedicated officers who served in the Founder's city — among them being Martha Field whose love for the needy had caught the imagination of the City Corporation.

But there was no need of new buildings to keep the memory of Martha Field alive in Nottingham, for it lives on in the minds and lives of so many people: policemen, ambulance drivers, doctors, nurses, social workers, and, of course, her own officer colleagues. Her name is a by-word for caring — remembered with affection and respect, not least, among her friends still living around Peel Street, or rehoused from the Storer Street area.

Many times during her years of service Martha had been asked — 'Would you do it again?' — 'Was it all worthwhile?' Her answer has always been the same. 'Yes — because I have seen wonderful help given to people through The Salvation Army, and found great opportunities for bringing Jesus Christ to people. *Yes — for God called me.*'